STRENGTH AND CONDITIONING FOR THE CHEER ATHLETE

A GUIDE TO IMPROVE PERFORMANCE AND REDUCE INJURY IN CHEERLEADING

Laura Turner, PT DPT CSFS

Strength and Conditioning for the Cheer Athlete

Strength and Conditioning for The Cheer Athlete

By Laura Turner

1st Edition

© 2024 Laura Turner

Published by Move Better

ISBN: 979-8-9985627-8-5

This book is not intended to be medical advice. Please seek assistance from your medical professional and get approval from your physician before starting any exercise program. The author and publisher are not liable for any injury or damages resulting from the application of the exercises or information in this book. The content is for informational purposes only and is not a substitute for professional medical advice.

Cover Design and Illustrations: Created by the author using Canva

Printed in the USA

Acknowledgments:

A special thank you to Keyonni Adams, the athlete in the videos, for your dedication and hard work.

Dedicated to my niece, Lexi Turner.

TABLE OF CONTENTS

Introduction..8

Cheer Lingo: Navigating The Playbook...........................23

Falls hurt. The cost of an injury...................................31

The Champion Mindset...44

Fueling For Performance...52

Unlocking Mobility, Flexibility, Strength, and Stability for Peak
Performance...59

Building the Foundation: Key Elements of a Strength &
Conditioning
Routine...62

Recharge to Perform: The Art of Rest and Recovery to Stay on the
Floor...67

Mirror Check: Mastering Self-Assessment for Peak
Performance...71

Strength in Motion: Exercises to Safeguard and Elevate Your
Performance...94

Blueprint for Success: Designing Effective Exercise Programs for
Cheer Athletes..109

Conclusion...128

Connect With Laura..130

Author's Note..131

I Couldn't Have Done This Without You..........................133

References..136

INTRODUCTION

Where do I start? I started cheerleading when I was 15 years old at Bethlehem Central High School, in Delmar, NY, just outside of Albany. When I look at where kids start now, I was old by today's standards, but it found me at just the right time. I had tried swimming and softball, but never really felt the pull. When my friends convinced me to try out for cheerleading in 10th grade, I finally felt like I had found my place. I loved being part of the team and even more standing on the sidelines and yelling cheers. We did climbing stunts such as shoulder sits and shoulder stands. We danced. We did herkies for jumps and cartwheels for our tumbling. The talented girls were able to do toe touches and 1-2 could do a back handspring. I didn't compete in high school, but cheerleading did get me points to get into the Girls Athletic Association, so even back in the early 1980's schools did consider us athletes. When a new coach came in the winter season of my senior year, I was excited because I could see the progress and change she would bring to the team. Sadly, I did not make the team. I can remember how devastated I felt and how much I wanted to tell the coach that I had made the team at Northeastern University (NU) the following year. It is amazing how driven by failure I still am.

Cheerleading at Northeastern changed my life. When I was on the field or court, I could relax and be myself. I really enjoyed the football and basketball games. It was so exciting when the team made a big play, and how we would throw up basket tosses or build pyramids to celebrate. I learned how to twist and flip in the air. Sadly, I never learned those skills on the ground. I was always scared after breaking my collarbone 3 times in my youth. My teammates became my closest friends, and we always hung out after games. We always had team dinners, at the restaurant on campus and we would share the wins and losses of the day. We became really close to our coach and knew she had our back. Whenever we had to do fundraising events, we would always find ways to laugh and knew we were in this thing called cheer together. This was what being part of a team meant to me. The camaraderie we shared while working towards a common goal: to be athletes, make friends and have fun along the way.

When I didn't make the basketball team after my second tryout (man, that tryout dance was tough!), I knew that I would come back and do better. The next football season I tried out and came in first place. Again, I am astonished at how failure has helped me achieve everything that is important to me.

Our hanging out after games eventually got me into trouble with school. As a physical therapy student, I really needed to spend more time studying than hanging out after games and practices. Gross Anatomy and Neurophysiology were my nemesis. The first time I took them, I earned a C-, which unfortunately wasn't enough to pass. While extremely disappointing, this allowed me to think about my priorities and what I wanted for my life.

I was able to do a longer co-op and figured out that if becoming a physical therapist (PT) was important to me, I would have to work harder. I was still able to cheer during that time because

I was technically still enrolled in school with the co-op program (and because I had to take two more anatomy courses to catch up.). Because both cheering and PT were important to me, I excelled and stayed cheering right until my senior year. I chose to stop cheering, after 4 full years on the teams, so that I could focus on my clinical affiliations. Northeastern was a 5-year PT program at the time because of co-op. Because I had to take that year off, I was in school for 6 years. Stopping cheerleading in my senior year was the right thing to do at the time, but to this day, I feel I missed out on that last year on the team.

Cheerleading in college was very different from high school. We had a full co-ed squad in college. We practiced outside and didn't use mats, but we did not think twice about it. Truthfully, practicing on the quad was a brilliant recruiting tactic by my coach. I think almost all the guys on our team walked by practice at one point and we were able to talk them into trying out. This was right at the beginning of our progressing to the strong team we became. Guys still had to try out so that they started the process of learning how to cheer. Most of them did not tumble and had no idea what stunting meant, but we loved teaching them. I look at some of my former teammates now and am amazed at what they went through to learn how to toss a girl in the air and catch her while she was flinging her arms around diving toward his head. And a lot of them also pushed themselves to learn how to do a back handspring because they knew it would be good for us on the competition floor. That took some serious guts!

My coach, Lorrie Wright, had a vision for our team. She always took us on 1-2 away trips per year. We went to Maine, New Hampshire, Connecticut, and even Buffalo. We would practice wherever we could: racquetball courts, ballrooms or outside. We went to Niagara Falls and Toronto. We danced on the sidelines and in our rooms. Lorrie had rules and curfews, but she treated us like adults, and we respected her for it.

In 1986, she took us to the Universal Cheerleaders Association (UCA) camp at Virginia Tech. We were in over our heads. We were with teams who were doing libs and flipping baskets. We were learning how to do toss chairs and pop up to shoulder stands. I remember being in awe of the team from the University of Kentucky. They were so put together. Even their lipstick matched. (Kentucky is still one of the top cheer teams to this day)

In 1987 we went to cheer camp at Rutgers University. Our team was progressing. We were able to keep up better and advance our skills. We made friends with more teams and acknowledged that we wanted to do the things that they were doing. We came back motivated to do more. I can still remember one 8-count of the dance to "Good Golly Miss Molly" by Little Richard (Richard, 1966), like it was yesterday.

In 1988, the National Cheerleaders Association held their first cheer camp at Boston University. Although we loved our road trips, it was nice to be able to just take a 10-minute van ride to camp. This is the year that I felt our team really took hold. We stayed out late practicing the routines we learned, and it paid off. We won The Spirit and Fight Song Awards, and we won our first bid to Nationals. Suddenly, our team transformed into a competition team. We hired a choreographer from Oklahoma, we stayed on campus over our winter break, and we didn't care. We learned how to torch flip and to build a high- chair. That first competition, in Dallas, Tx, we were like deer in headlights. Nearly every stunt came down. When it was time to torch flip, I missed the count, flipped late, and my partner had already moved on…luckily, we had mats, and I just bounced up and on to the next formation. Mishaps happen in cheerleading under the best of circumstances. We were disappointed with our 13th finish, but we knew we would be back.

The following summer we were aiming not only for a bid, but for the elite title of camp champ, and we got both. We had several (not me) team members get an application to be on NCA staff. We put Northeastern on the map for cheerleading, and it was amazing! This year we hired James Speed, who was the coach of Kansas at the time, as our choreographer. He then moved on to coach at Louisville, another powerhouse cheer team. James instilled confidence in us, and we loved our routine. He even had me attempting a handspring with a spot…man I wish I had been able to get over my fear. We had more tumbling and flipping in our routine. Our dance was inspired by Dirty Dancing and Blue Ocean, by New Order. We practiced primarily in the Ell Center Ballroom and very often in classrooms with roll away mats. When the competition rolled around, again in Dallas, we were ready. We went out with confidence and took seventh place. We were beyond thrilled because we had beaten our goal, we had a solid routine, and we loved being together as a team. I was captain for basketball season, and I was so proud of my team. I wish I had been able to express just how much I admired all of them. To this day, we have remained friends and still chuckle about our antics throughout our time together.

Lorrie frequently asked fellow alumni to come back, and judge tryouts and I jumped at the chance whenever I could. I loved watching the team progress and grow. They finally got solid practice space in the gymnastic room, in Cabot gym. I would go to watch the cheerleaders perform at high school competitions and at regional competitions in Albany. I wish I had been around when they were asked to perform at the 1996 Olympic opening ceremonies. What an honor! I stayed in close contact with Lorrie and the team and was so excited when I was able to travel to see them compete in 2002 in Daytona. There is seriously no better feeling than to watch your coach win a Grand National Championship and to see the incredible feats this team now could do. Yes. My Husky Pride runs deep. These kids were AMAZING.

I was out of college for 6 years before cheerleading called my name again. I contacted Watertown High School to see if they wanted help with their cheer team and suddenly, I was into coaching. The coach was rarely at practice. I think the girls were excited to have someone present who knew more current cheerleading, and who wanted to help them progress. I loved every moment. The prior coach ended up leaving after a year, and I was promoted to head coach. It was a whole new world. Not only was I not ON the sidelines, but I was responsible for these kids' safety. We started going to camp and bringing in choreographers to improve our competition skills. I soon realized that coaching was more than just skill development. In my first 2.5 years of coaching, I learned just how hard it was to be a teenager at that time. One girl was hospitalized for anorexia, which I never saw coming. After missing a season, she was able to return, and I vowed that I would make sure my team knew how important food was to fuel our body. Another girl had cystic fibrosis and would frequently miss practice because she was hospitalized. I admired how she always pushed herself while at practice and I hope being part of a team helped her through those tough times. The biggest 'injury' that I remember during that time was a girl on my newly formed junior varsity (JV) team. We were practicing thigh stands outside, and she stepped off and into a hole. She sustained a tibial fracture that kept her out the rest of the year.

I can remember getting frustrated with the entire team when we were preparing for a competition or a pep rally because they were being silly and distracted. Looking back, I should have embraced the play and set more time boundaries for being serious. It is important for kids to be able to be silly at times. And it is more important when trying new skills or pushing yourself to hit a routine, to be focused on what you are doing.

I left Watertown because I bought a house in Northborough, MA and it was about an hour away. The high school in my new town, Algonquin Regional High School, was looking for a head coach, and the team was very competitive. They even had an established coed team in the winter season. I was so excited because this is what I learned from Northeastern. I had two assistant coaches and a JV team as well. I remember being at our first league competition and the mother of a former team member walked by me and said that our team would never be able to compete at the same level as they did before I started coaching. That hurt…and my team proved her wrong over the next 3 years. Her second daughter started cheering for me 2 years later, and all 3 of us are still friendly to this day.

My Algonquin team was focused. They were used to strength and conditioning in the summer, and I think they looked forward to it. They wanted to win at competitions and although they had only competed in the winter as a coed team before, were excited to try competing as an all-girl team in the fall. We consistently were in the top 5 in our division, and I saw both teams continue to progress. It was my dream for them to continue to cheer in college because I knew what a special time I had cheering at NU. And I'm happy to say that quite a few did make that transition to college cheer or dance.

At ARHS we had our own drama and learning curves too. I had two girls with juvenile diabetes, and it made me realize again how important nutrition was to stay healthy and active. One girl was diagnosed while on the team, and I never realized how much it may have affected her attitude. I had always tried to instill teamwork, a positive attitude and cheering from the heart. This girl and I would butt heads almost daily for a year. Ultimately, the butting heads made me decide to leave. This was a decision I always regretted, because these kids had a piece of my own heart. I never knew just what she was going through until after I left Algonquin, and I'm happy to say she and I had a heart to heart later. She's doing amazing now, and she continued to cheer, with blood sugar under control, after I was gone.

I do not remember any catastrophic injuries at ARHS. Someone dislocated a finger coming out of a stunt. There were a few rolled ankles and shoulder tweaks. Some had low back pain. I was lucky to have a Certified Athletic Trainer, on site full-time, who always treated us the same as the other athletes. I was also extremely lucky to have an Athletic Director, who considered us a normal sports team. He always helped us find practice space and made sure we had mats to practice on. I still think he was the best boss I ever had. His parting words to me as I left that head coach position were "You are a truly kind person. When you coach, you need to come in with strict rules and stick to them. Later, you might bend them a little, but always start off strictly." I wish I had followed his advice.

I had no intention of continuing to coach after I left Algonquin, but soon I was bored with just doing PT and I saw an opening at The College of the Holy Cross which was 10 minutes from my house. Back in college cheerleading I jumped!

Coaching at Cross, I finally realized what a God send parents were for a cheer coach. At the high schools, the parents always helped and ran our fundraisers. Our money went for the end of the year awards. In college, we had to raise money for uniforms, and to get mats to use for practice. We sold t-shirts and candy to help us go to Nationals. We had to rearrange our practices in the winter so that we could find practice space. And as was the norm in the cheer world, our cheerleaders were mostly used at games to promote marketing events. I agree with this. It makes sense that the people who are working to get people to make some noise would be the ones to toss t-shirts into the crowd and to cheer on the fans who were competing in 3-point contests or those marshmallow men bumper games. Cheerleaders (and dance teams too) work hard to create excitement at a game and at the same time work hard to promote the school.

In the six years that I coached at Holy Cross we had a few big injuries. I believe many injuries in cheerleading occur because the athletes are tired, not ready to advance a skill, or because they are distracted. Yes, traumatic injuries do occur that are flukes, but most big injuries happen due to preparedness. We did have access to the Athletic Training (AT) department at Cross and they were great, but they were not always on site where we practiced, and that is where most of our injuries occurred. I took 2 cheerleaders to the emergency room. One, who also had a knee injury prior to coming to Cross, went via ambulance because she couldn't stand or walk on her leg. She had a tibial plateau fracture after landing wrong out of a stunt. The other had a broken nose after being clocked while catching a cradle. I am sure we had a few back and ankle sprains/strains along the way, but those two injuries stand out to me. I am not sure we could have prevented them, but I do think having a safe and consistent space to practice, which was near the Athletic Training Department, may have helped more.

One of the best decisions we made as a team was to begin a strength and conditioning (S&C) program. The S&C coaches welcomed us into the weight room with open arms. Yes, the team had to work out at off times, but they programmed for us and treated us like any other athlete. I think the team really liked it too. We had less injuries that year and I could see an advancement in their ability to stunt and tumble. I wish we had started the process sooner because I know for sure that cross training and strength work help to make better athletes with less risk of injury.

The downside to my coaching in 2009, 19 years after I cheered, was that I was no longer able to demonstrate the stunts that they were doing. I brought in other coaches to continue to help, but my team got frustrated. I also expected them to be around for breaks because we had games, and although I still wanted to compete, I just did not sense the commitment that was needed to do a safe routine. I started to realize that cheerleading at Cross was different from Northeastern. There was much more focus on academics- a lot of my team members went on to med school or law school- and on community service. I admired how committed they were to these other activities, even though it didn't fit with what my vision for the team was. My team confronted me in frustration mid-way through the winter season. They wanted to be doing more and didn't feel that I was helping them enough. My boss told me I should kick them all off and start over the following season. That didn't sit right with me, so I walked away. I had never quit a job (or a team) mid-way through before. It made me sad. Looking back, I think it was just time. I was able to reconnect with the girls later, and I think in the long run, they were happier and able to progress more. And it spurred me to reconnect with my husband after many years of coaching and being absent.

In December 2009 I got pregnant. I was ridiculously happy. I looked back and thought how much time I had lost waiting while I coached. Then in March of 2010, I miscarried. I was devastated. I was older and knew I did not have another chance. For the next 6 months, I struggled to even get out of bed. When a former cheerleader called and asked me to be her assistant back at Algonquin, I felt like I could start to breathe again. When she left the following year, I stayed to coach the JV team. It felt right to be back coaching, but boy! There was a difference in maturity level at 14 than at 16. It taught me more about how teenagers grow through the years. We sustained 5 concussions that year due to head butts and falls. I was trying to allow the girls to progress when they did not have the body control nor the attention span at the time. I know they were frustrated but given our injury rate, I also knew I could not let them do more until they were ready. I also knew it was time to say when. This time I finished the season and left with a clear conscience, knowing that my tenure as a coach had come to an end.

In 2013 I decided to return to school for my Doctorate in Physical Therapy. After 21 years, I knew I needed to learn more if I was going to stay in the field for the duration. As part of our degree, we had to do a Comprehensive Case Analysis. I had planned on doing it on an assessment/treatment technique that I had been studying but really did not have enough content to create a good case. Finally, I realized that I could combine an analysis of the Functional Movement Screen with cheerleading. It felt like I had come full circle.

Being a cheerleader helped me in so many ways. I made friends. I became part of a team. I recognized the benefits of moving my body versus just going home and being a couch potato after school. I cheered for football and basketball for 4 years of college. I learned that I needed to push myself if I wanted to achieve anything. I was able to travel with my teammates and my coach and I got to see more of the USA than I ever would have had I not cheered. When I struggled in school, I learned that if I wanted to stay on the team, I needed to step up my study habits. I started to learn that I could stand in front of a crowd and not feel like I should crawl back into my shy little hole.

I started coaching a few years after I graduated. Suddenly I was responsible for people in a way I never had been before, or since. As a physical therapist, I always looked at the potential for injury. As a coach, I fought that with a need to push my team to achieve more. I recognize now that the athletes I coached gave me so much more than I could have ever imagined. Despite the name calling on a bus, the despair I felt as they told me I was a bad coach, and the struggles we went through in becoming adults, these athletes filled a void that I missed out on. I realize now that they taught me a little of what being a parent was like. I loved watching them grow up and I love watching them become parents and grown-ups now. I cherish every single moment.

When I left coaching in 2012, I thought my journey with cheerleading was over. Little did I know it was just the beginning. To say cheerleading molded who I am is an understatement. It became my whole identity. And now, I can focus on helping cheerleaders to stay healthy. To improve their skills by teaching them to move better and get stronger. To help them stay on the floor and continue to do what they love for as long as they want.

My intent with this book is to provide a framework to help parents, coaches, and cheerleaders to be able to address potential risk of injury; to recognize what mobility, stability and strength are really needed to perform well; and to outline a start point to help train in the off-season. While my experience has only been with high school and college athletes, the content is applicable to all cheerleaders.

I do not believe that we can prevent all injuries. That is part of the nature and risk of any sport. I do believe that we can reduce the risk by learning how to move better, by being fully present when we are at work, and by recognizing when we need to take a break. I hope you find some value and continue to push yourself to be better and learn from your mistakes. After all, that is what makes us human. Cheers to you for taking the initiative!

How to use this book

The first chapters of this book will provide a framework for reducing injuries and why it's important to look at the whole body when creating strength and conditioning programs. While this book is not intended to teach and improve specific cheer skills, the material will enhance all. Learning why you need to improve your mobility as well as strength, and how that happens through your body will allow you to understand what you're doing with a specific exercise. Being able to see and feel what your body is doing will help you to do it more effectively and will inherently be safer and you'll progress faster.

If you don't wish to learn the why, jump straight to The Blueprint for Success. This is where the specific exercises begin. Here we will start with a self-assessment so that you can choose the exercises that will be specific for you. There are exercises to include in a warm-up, strength and agility exercises and finally conditioning exercises.

The Lingo

As we move forward with learning how to reduce the risk of injuries in cheerleading, I think it's important to know basic anatomy and to understand some medical as well as cheer lingo. Different cheer programs call stunts something different, even though the technique is the same. These are my definitions.

A. Anatomy

a. Lumbar Spine-the lower back from below the ribs to just below the pelvis. There are 5 lumbar vertebrae.

b. Cervical Spine-the neck. There are 7 cervical vertebrae.

c. Thoracic Spine-the mid back. There are 12 thoracic vertebrae which connect to the 12 ribs.

d. Pelvis-the bones that connect the spine to the lower body.

e. Anterior Superior Iliac Spine (ASIS)- Front bony prominence on the pelvis

f. Posterior Superior Iliac Spine (PSIS)-Back bony prominence on the pelvis

g. The sternum-center of the chest joins with the ribs.

h. Talus-the ankle bone that connects the lower leg to the foot.

i. Calcaneus-heel bone

j. Tarsals-5 mid foot bones that join with the metatarsals.

k. Metatarsals-5-long foot bones that join with the phalanges (toes) called the metatarsal phalangeal joint (MTP); the big toe is called 1st and pinkie toe is 5th.

l. Metatarsal head-the knuckle of the toes.

m. Transverse Abdominis (TVA)-deep core muscle that runs from the ribs to the pelvis; actions to flex, laterally flex and rotate the trunk to the same side; assists with exhalation.

n. Internal Abdominal Oblique (IAO)-lateral abdominal core muscle that attaches to the ribs and pelvis. Action-flex, laterally flex and rotate to the same side. Helps with exhalation.

o. External Abdominal Oblique (EAO)-lateral abdominal core muscle that attaches from the upper ribs to the pelvis; assists with exhalation.

p. Multifidus-deep spinal muscles that run from the low back to the head. Extends (moves backwards) and rotates the spine; Assists with exhalation.

q. Erector spinae-spinal muscles that run the length of the spine.

r. Quadratus lumborum-runs from ribs to pelvis. Extends spine, laterally flexes, and rotates to the same side.

s. Hip flexors-front of thigh.

    i. Psoas-flexes and externally rotates the hip; runs from upper lumbar spine to front of upper leg.

    ii. Iliacus-flexes hip; runs along the inside of the pelvic crest.

    iii. Rectus Femoris-flexes hip and extends knee. Starts at ASIS, attaches with other quads below the knee.

t. Hip Adductors-inner thigh; there are 5 muscles. All work to bring the leg towards midline while assisting with flexion and internal rotation. The adductor magnus also acts as a 4th hamstring.

    i. Pectineus

    ii. Brevis

    iii. Longus

    iv. Magnus

    v. Gracilis

u. Glutes

i. Maximus-largest muscle in the back of the leg; attaches at the posterior ilium, PSIS, Thoracolumbar aponeurosis, sacrum, coccyx, Sacrotuberous ligament and gluteal aponeurosis and runs to the gluteal tuberosity and iliotibial band; extends, abducts, and externally rotates the hip via the upper portion; flexes and internally rotates to slow trunk forward movement.

ii. Medius-top to side of hip; anterior gluteal line of ilium to lateral surface of greater trochanter; internally rotates and abducts hip; maintains upright trunk by stabilizing the pelvis, when standing on one leg.

iii. Minimus-attaches at the anterior and inferior gluteal lines of ilium and the greater sciatic notch and the greater trochanter and posterior hip joint capsule; abducts the hip; anterior portion flexes and internally rotates; posterior portion extends and externally rotates the hip. (Dooley, Folckomer, & Quirk, 2019)

v. Ligaments-attach bone to bone

w. Tendons-attach muscle to bone

B. Movement Definitions

    a. Anterior: front

    b. Posterior: back

    c. Lateral: side

    d. Sagittal plane: front to back

    e. Frontal plane: side to side

    f. Transverse plane: rotation

    g. Dorsiflexion: top of foot moves toward shin

    h. Plantarflexion: bottom of foot moves down (pointing toes)

    i. Inversion: Foot turns in

    j. Eversion: Foot turns out

    k. Flexion: Sagittal plane motion moving forward

    l. Extension: Sagittal plane motion moving backward

    m. Abduction: Frontal plane motion moving away from the body

    n. Adduction: Frontal plane motion moving toward the center of the body

o. Supination: palm of hand or sole of foot turns up; in the foot it is a combination of inversion and plantarflexion

p. Pronation: palm of hand or sole of foot turns down; in the foot it is a combination of eversion and dorsiflexion

C. Cheerleading Definitions

a. Flyer-top person

b. Main base-primary support under the flyer

c. Side base-secondary support under the flyer

d. Back-back support

e. Spot-extra person to catch if a flyer comes down.

f. Half (extension)- the flyer is on 2 legs and bases hold with their hands at shoulder height.

g. Full (extension)-flyer is held above the base's head on 2 feet.

h. Liberty-flyer is held above the base's head on one-foot, opposite foot at knee height.

i. Heel stretch-flyer is held above the base's head on one-foot with the opposite leg held out to the side.

j. Arabesque-flyer is held above the base's head on one foot with the opposite leg extended behind at about waist high.

k. Scorpion-flyer is held above the base's head on one foot with the opposite foot held over the head.

l. Scale-flyer is held above the base's head on one foot, like an arabesque, but with the back leg held at the knee.

m. Back handspring-gymnastics tumbling where the person flips backwards landing with hands on the ground, springing over until the feet land.

n. Back tuck-tumbling in which the person flips backward without hands touching the ground, knees tucked in and lands on feet.

When I was coaching at Algonquin, a judge at a competition commented on our routine "falls hurt." That always stuck with me. At first, I was annoyed, thinking she meant our scores. I mean, duh! Of course, falls hurt, but they are also common in the cheer world. You work so that they don't happen in a competition or in a game, but they are going to happen. It is part of the nature of learning a new skill. The difference is, falls don't have to be injurious, if we are prepared. When we are not prepared, mentally and physically, injuries from mild to severe can and do occur. In this chapter, we'll go over some common injuries that occur in cheerleading. In subsequent chapters, we'll discuss ways to reduce the risk.

When an injury occurs, there may be associated pain. Conversely, someone may have pain, but not have an injury. They may have just a mechanical change that can be corrected easily. Pain and injury can lead to time out of practice or competition. It can contribute to time out of school. It may limit time spent with friends. When someone is injured, they may be cranky at home, thus affecting family relationships. When not treated or addressed and improved depression and anxiety can set in. Injuries may be minor, but they can have catastrophic effects on an athlete's well-being. Falls really do hurt.

Common Cheerleading Injuries: My research in 2016 (Laura Turner & Jeananne Elkins, 2016) showed that most cheerleading injuries occurred during practice. This may have been for lack of proper equipment, poor supervision, or likely that cheerleaders were learning new skills. Generally, on the sidelines or on a competition mat, people are performing the skills they can do solidly. In practice is where cheerleaders try new things and sometimes injury will occur. Learning a new skill to mastery involves error at times. It's how our brain learns: make a mistake, try again until the correct movement is achieved. And then do it again and again and again. At this point, fatigue sets in and more injuries are likely to occur. Being aware of when this is happening is one important way to reduce overall injuries.

Traumatic vs overuse injuries There are two common ways that injuries occur. Either by a traumatic event such as a fall, trip, or a collision. Or due to overuse. Overuse injuries are defined by the Mayo clinic as "a muscle or joint injury, such as tendonitis or a stress fracture, that occurs due to repetitive trauma. Training errors can occur when someone does too much too fast and therefore strains the muscles/tendons/bones and leads to overuse. Technique errors occur when someone has poor form and thus creates abnormal stress on the structures, again leading to overuse." (Staff, 2019)

Ankle Sprains The research found that the most common injury in cheerleading was an ankle sprain. (Laura Turner & Jeananne Elkins, 2016) These generally occurred in All-star cheerleaders when coming out of a tumbling pass or if someone stepped off the mat wrong. A lateral, (or outside) ankle sprain generally happens when the foot rolls in, and the outside of the ankle rolls out. Healthcare professionals grade the sprains on a scale of 1-3 where 1 is mild, 2 a little more severe, and 3 there is a complete tear of the ligament. Ligaments provide feedback to our brain that helps to determine where our bones are in space. When ligaments are overstretched, they signal the brain to stop the motion, and our bones course correct to prevent a fall or a tear. When we roll our ankle too far it will create this tear in the ligament. When ligaments are torn it will create pain and swelling which will then limit the movement in the ankle. If the swelling lingers (becomes chronic) it will contribute to decreased strength of the muscles that help to do the movement of the bones. Ligaments can heal if they are outside a capsule, which they are in the ankle, but they never regain their full contractile properties, therefore restoring normal motion of the joints. Increasing the strength of the muscles to help support the ligament function is crucial to preventing further injury. While someone may be able to 'shake it off' after a mild sprain, and to continue practicing, it's still important to work on restoring that motion and strength. When the rehab isn't done after a sprain, it can lead to compensation further up the body, such as the knee and hip. If this person is a flyer, they may have difficulty holding single leg stunts. If they're a tumbler, they may have difficulty in landing a pass. If they're a base, they may compensate by stepping out and losing their balance just a little...which we all know can lead to the other people in the stunts demise.

After an ankle sprain, an athlete may be able to continue to practice or perform, but initially they may need to wear a brace to allow the tissue to heal. As the joint heals, pain decreases, and swelling goes down and a brace may not be needed. It's not uncommon to reinjure a ligament, and usually the subsequent time is worse than the first. The worse the tear, the bigger the need for outside stability, but again, rehab and consistent work to maintain the joint integrity can help to prevent a bigger injury such as a fracture which would require a longer time out of practice. Yes, ankle sprains are a relatively benign injury. However, if not managed properly, this traumatic injury can lead to repetitive strain injuries, and bigger traumatic injuries.

Ankle sprains can be reduced by working on normalizing joint mechanics and by assuring good supporting strength around the ankle, hip, and core. A brace may be helpful to allow a cheerleader to stay in the game but doing work to build mobility and strength will prevent further injury. Ankle sprains may be relatively benign (unless there is a fracture along with it) but if left untreated, a flyer will compensate with their pelvis, hips, or core to stabilize; a base may not be able to set correctly or will have difficulty staying under the flyer for small corrections; these may lead to bigger injuries should a fall occur.

Back Injuries Low back injuries were the second biggest injuries. The lower back can be injured either by a traumatic injury, such as a spinal fracture that leads to a spinal cord injury (thankfully, these appear to be few in the cheer world), or by chronic overuse leading to weakened muscles and sprained ligaments which can contribute to things such as bulging or herniated discs. Herniated and bulging discs sometimes require surgery, depending on the degree of pressure the disc is putting on the nerve, and what the limitations are. Most can be managed by improving movement and stability.

Postural changes such as increased lordosis along with repeated hyperextension movements, without proper anterior core control can lead to a sprain of the supporting ligaments in the back, a strain of the muscles that support the back, spondylosis (degenerative spinal changes), a spondylolysis (a fracture of the pars interarticularis, which is a small section of a vertebrae which connects the facets (Spine-health.com, 2020)) or a spondylolisthesis (a slipping forward of one vertebrae on the one below). These injuries are not catastrophic in diagnosis and are generally manageable with exercise and movement correction.

I find that a lot of cheerleaders will 'work through' back and neck pain. Only when it gets severe will they seek help. However, if they get therapeutic help early on, they may prevent a worse injury and thus time out of cheer.

High Hamstring Pulls The hamstrings are a group of 3 muscles. They all have a proximal attachment to the ischial tuberosity otherwise known as the "sit" bones. The Bicep Femoris has 2 heads, the long head attaches at the ischial tuberosity and the short head attaches at the lateral lip of the

Linea aspera. The distal attachment is at the fibula, the bone on the outside of your lower leg. The Semimembranosus and Semi-tendinosis attach distally to the medial tibial condyle, on the inside of the knee.

The Bicep femoris flexes and laterally rotates the knee as well as extends the hip. The Semi-tendinosis flexes and medially rotates the knee and extends the hip. The Semimembranosus flexes the knee and extends the hip.

The Adductor Magnus also has an attachment to the ischial tuberosity. It helps with hip extension, adduction, and medial rotation. This is the area injured when one has a high hamstring pull.

Hamstring pulls occur when the muscles are strained. They may occur with high impact activities such as running or jumping. There can be a feeling of a 'pop' and sharp pain when it initially occurs. The pain is usually right at the "sit" bone but may also be down the back of the leg. Sometimes bruising will occur. Most mild pulls will resolve quickly with rest and gentle stretching. If the pain is lingering, it's important to follow up with a physician and to start physical therapy.

In the clinic, I have found the adductor magnus and hamstrings to be overworking and compensating for the rectus femoris, a quad muscle that flexes the hip and extends the knee. For these compensations, we massage the adductor magnus and hamstrings, usually at the site of pain, and gently work on lengthening or dynamic stretching followed by an exercise to strengthen the rectus femoris.

Because the hamstrings, and adductor magnus, attach at the ischial tuberosity of the pelvis, I also find it common to have decreased core stability. Either the lower back or abdominals may be underworking and this decrease in stability will contribute to an overuse of the hamstrings. Creating better mobility-aka flexibility and reflexive stability-around the core is important in fully recovering from a high hamstring pull. This may involve proper breathing techniques or spinal mobility exercises. Gradually progressing to standing weight shifting in the phases of gait and incorporating 3 planes of movement can be a big benefit and are easy to do anywhere. Once resting pain is resolved, and mobility is improving, adding resistance exercises for the core such as will help keep the core strong.

Knee injuries Common knee injuries that are seen in cheerleaders range from patella tendonitis (pain in the front of the knee due to overuse); Anterior Cruciate Ligament (ACL) and medial collateral ligament (MCL) tears; and meniscal injuries.

The ACL connects the thigh bone (femur) to the shin bone (tibia). It prevents the tibia from sliding forward on the femur in full extension(straight) and full flexion (bent). ACL injuries tend to be traumatic in nature due to planting the foot and pivoting on an extended knee. In cheerleading, ACL injuries may also occur via tumbling mishaps, or poor landing technique on jumps and stunts. Females tend toward hyperextension of our knees which puts added strain on the ACL. The MCL prevents the knee from too much medial (towards center) translation. This can be sprained or torn in conjunction with the ACL. Although it is possible to function without an ACL, it does not heal on its own and will generally require surgical repair. The MCL can heal, but as with ankle sprains, it never regains its full stability and requires more assistance from surrounding muscles to provide stability. ACL reconstruction surgery and rehab lasts 6-12 months. The movement and strength must return, and the joint must heal before any running and jumping can occur and this is usually about 16-20 weeks. At around 24 weeks, cutting, pivoting and agility drills can start. It's quite common for females to either injure the opposite ACL or to reinjure the same one. Long term strength and mobility work will help to prevent reinjury.

There are two menisci in the knee. The medial meniscus is on the inside of the knee and lateral on the outside. They are located between the femur and tibia and provide added stability to the knee and a bit of shock absorption. Rotational forces at the knee, either on an extended knee, or at end range of flexion may contribute to a meniscal tear. While these may require surgical repair, it is possible to rehab a meniscus injury without surgery. The need for repair may be determined by pain management and general stability of the knee. In the under 25 population, a meniscus may be repaired and stitched together. Otherwise, they remove the piece of meniscus which is called a meniscectomy. The meniscal repair requires limited weight bearing in the initial 4-6 weeks, and general limitations on end range of motion. While the initial rehab is longer (6 months to a year), it may preserve the integrity of the joint space between the femur and the tibia thus leading to less problems down the road. If someone undergoes a meniscectomy, they are generally able to return to sport after 6-8 weeks but will likely need to do more maintenance work to prevent further injury.

Shoulder and upper body injuries Traumatic upper body injuries that may occur are shoulder and finger subluxations and dislocations. These may occur when a flyer comes down 'wrong' and the base attempts to catch on an outstretched arm. Dislocations and subluxations are when a joint is displaced. Someone who has had repeated dislocations may be subject to recurrent subluxations. Beyond the obvious pain that occurs, the shoulder becomes less stable. A good rehab program that corrects stability around the shoulder joint can limit reinjury. If someone is constantly reinjuring that same structure, they may require surgery to improve overall stability. After surgery, mobility is limited in the first 8 weeks to let the tissues heal, at which point further strength training can occur. This too, is a long recovery process, but can help prevent long term instability issues if addressed early.

The glenoid labrum is the cartilage of the shoulder joint. It helps to provide joint stability and deepens the glenohumeral socket. The glenohumeral joint is the connection between the shoulder blade (glenoid fossa) and the humeral head (top of the upper arm). The labrum is one of the attachments for the long head of the bicep. Injuries to the labrum can occur because of a dislocation and with heavy weight being held overhead. (Physical Therapy Guide to shoulder Labral tear., 2011) The need for surgical intervention depends on the degree of functional loss. Managing pain, returning mobility, and increasing strength is something that can be done in therapy to avoid surgery in some cases.

The rotator cuff is a group of four muscles: supraspinatus, infraspinatus, teres minor and subscapularis. They rotate and glide the humerus down in the socket, called the glenoid fossa. They work together with the muscles of the scapula (shoulder blade) and the bigger muscles of the arm (deltoids, pectorals, bicep) when we raise our arm. Because the glenoid fossa is not that deep, the rotator cuff helps to provide stability along with the ligaments and labrum (cartilage). Traumatic rotator cuff tears may occur from a fall on an outstretched arm, catching a flyer 'wrong' or in conjunction with a dislocation. Rotator cuff tendonitis occurs when the rotator cuff is overworking or underworking in relation to another supporting muscle. This can lead to irritation and possible formation of bone spurs. Correcting abnormal movement patterns and muscle imbalances can prevent a tear from overuse. Rotator cuff surgery entails limiting motion for about 8 weeks, avoiding active use of the arm for 8 weeks, and gradual progression and strength training. To achieve full active range of motion and strength can take a good year.

It is possible to return to cheerleading after shoulder surgery, but it will take a long time. Things like tendonitis or muscle strains may be ok to work through and to continue participating as pain allows. The trouble will present if the injury is worked beyond its capability or if pain becomes severe mid-stunt/tumble. Without proper strength and mobility, a base/back spot may put their flyer at risk for a worse injury. A flyer may be hesitant to push off or catch herself, causing the bases to have to absorb more. A tumbler may not be able to push out of their shoulders and face plant mid handspring. The good news is most of this is fixable with proper corrective exercise learned through a qualified medical professional.

Concussions These could arguably be the number one injury to cheerleaders now. In 2016 the research didn't show that, but I do believe concussions have been on the rise. "Concussions are a brain injury that occurs because of a bump, blow, or jolt to the head. They can also occur from a fall or a blow to the body that causes the head to move back and forth rapidly." (US Dept of Health and Human Services, 2010) Repeated concussions can lead to serious changes in brain function. The difficulty with a concussion is the symptoms may not be obvious. It was once thought that you only had a concussion if you lost consciousness. Today we know that even a mild injury can contribute to bigger issues.

Signs that your cheerleader may have a concussion are headaches, blurred vision, difficulty concentrating, dizziness, vertigo, and nausea. In the clinic, I see a lot of neck tension that goes along with a concussion. Symptoms may occur later than the actual injury as well. Anytime someone hits their head or falls and lands with enough impact to shake their head, it's important to monitor for signs of concussion for at least a few days.

If the brain is not allowed to heal before another impact occurs, long term memory and mood changes may occur. There have been multiple professional ball players who have committed suicide or acts of violence that have contributed to a history of concussions. Balance may be off either directly because of injury to the cerebellum or because of vestibular dysfunction affected by vision and the inner ear. The younger someone is at the time of their first concussion, the bigger the risk. For this reason, getting assessed by a Certified Athletic Trainer, a physician who specializes in head trauma and a physical therapist who specializes in concussion management is important. They may also be referred to a psychologist/psychiatrist to help with signs of depression that can occur in the recovery process.

Conclusion:

Healing from an injury is never a linear experience. Listening to your body and knowing when to increase or decrease an activity will be important. Too often I see people return to full participation in a sport before they are ready, and they reinjure themselves and take a step backwards. Remember to walk before you run, start with lower level plyometrics before powering into a full jumping routine. Regain flexibility along with stability before really pushing jump height or speed. If you respect the process, that pain in the butt will resolve and you may even be better overall for it too.

THE CHAMPION MINDSET

"I think I can, I think I can." (Piper, 1930) This classic line from the children's book "The Little Engine that could" is what we all need in our head when we are learning and struggling with a new skill. It's what goes through my head every time I ride my bike up a big hill. It also was my mantra when I was trying out for cheerleading each time.

Mindset is the key to any athletic activity, yet so many of us don't truly see how amazing we are both on and off the field. We struggle to learn something new, and we decide we just can't do it, so we give up. When I was a child, I broke my collarbone THREE times. The first time I was 6 and was doing a cartwheel on wet grass and slipped. The second time I was 9 and in gym class trying a front handspring and rolled wrong. I was 12 the third time I was doing a front walkover in my backyard and my arm gave out in my handstand. When the doctor told me that I wouldn't be able to wear strapless dresses if I broke it again. I told myself right then that I just couldn't do gymnastics. Fast forward to when my college team was prepping for Nationals, and I could never get over that fear and belief that I just couldn't tumble. It cost my team some points, and I have carried with me regret that I never pushed myself to learn that skill.

"Do or do not. There is no Try." Yoda (Lucas, Kasdan, & Yoda, 1980)

When we are met with obstacles that get in our way of achieving our goals, we have a choice. Give up and give in or use the obstacle to pave a new way. If you struggle with your tumbling, what is getting in the way? Mobility? Strength? Timing? What do you need to do to improve on any of those that you haven't already been doing? If a stunt isn't hitting, what is stopping you? This goes for trusting your partners too. If you don't believe that they can perform the stunt, that they will do their very best to catch you, or that your flyer will work to get and keep a stunt up, you likely won't master that new stunt. If you're a coach or a parent and don't believe that your team will succeed, they most certainly will not. "Whatever your mind can conceive, it can achieve." Napoleon Hill (Hill, 1937)

Mindset and belief come about from personal growth. We aren't wired to believe in ourselves. We need to work at it and continue to improve all the time. There are rules for constant growth and learning. which I think are key for mindset in cheerleading. These are (Larson, 2020):

1. Stop chasing shiny things. We all want to win that championship and get the rings and trophies, but what is more important is the process of getting there. The bonding with our team. The ability to learn a new skill and the fitness we attain in the process. The knowledge that we can put together some cool routines and execute to the best of our ability. The fun we have along the way. When we focus on the fundamentals of learning and building, we get more solid and have less injuries. When

our foundation is strong, we are limitless. Focus on all these fundamentals and stop focusing on the bling. In the end, you'll get so much more.

2. Do the work! If you do the work, you will see what really matters. Practice and choreography are only a piece of what will decrease your risk of injury. You need to work on your general fitness as well. You need to take the time to build trust with your teammates. And you need to focus and listen so that you know exactly what to do.

3. Be hungry. No. Not physically hungry. That's a recipe for disaster when you're cheering. Be hungry for improvement. Be hungry to learn. Be hungry to go after what you want. If you do so, your coach and team will do the same.

4. Don't use your past or current situations as an excuse. Yes, injuries may need some love to improve from (go back to number 2). But holding on to the memory of an old injury will stop you from moving forward. Taking your 'bad day' into practice will create drama throughout the practice. Speak your mind before you start and then LET IT GO! Find someone on your team to call you out when you do this, and you will keep making progress.

5. Be polite to the naysayers. There will be people in life who tell you that you cannot do something and sometimes they will be nasty in the process. Listen and process what they're saying, and then politely prove them wrong. If you need to rehab an injury, work through it, and get stronger. If you want to progress to the next level,

politely say thank you for your feedback, and then go do what it takes to progress. When you're heading into tryouts or to competition, shake your opponent's hand and wish them well. You will be remembered more for your kind gestures than for your skills on the mat or field. Make your team and your practices a haven for positive thoughts and behaviors and you will achieve so much more.

6. Only compare you to you. You cannot control what anyone else does. Whether it's a teammate or another team, or even another person with the 'same' injury. No injury is the same. We are all individuals and the only timeline for healing is the one that is yours. If you hit a new stunt or tumbling pass, applaud yourself wherever that may be. Don't let someone else who may have a different skill mastered cloud your achievement. Get inspired by another person's success and keep moving forward toward your next goal. "Keep calm and prove them wrong."

7. Get successful with your own time. When you are home, you have the choice to sit and watch Tik-Tok videos all day, or to practice and start to visualize the goal you are aiming for. If you're injured, time out is the perfect time to work on other body parts. Or to plan for your return. Maybe you don't have a personal goal. This is the time to get one and to imagine it like it's already happened. When you return, you will have a much easier time achieving a

new skill and you will see bigger progress-with less injury risk- because of it.

8. Go after it! Act even if you fail. Maybe you can't throw a scale double-down just yet, but can you do a scale on the ground? What do you need to do to make THAT happen? Now go get it. Can't participate in practice because you are injured, but still want to be in the routine? Be the first person at practice and take notes. Learn the material and see yourself doing it and you will have an easier time when you're ready to jump back in. While you're at it, do your rehab exercises, and then ask for more. Acting even if it's not perfect yet, will get you much bigger results...except when it comes to skill progression. That I believe that perfection before progression is super important ☺

9. Don't freak out on the clock but use the clock to push you. Yes, there is a time limit for entering a competition, but staying patient, and pushing yourself to be 1% better every day will help you continue positive progress vs losing traction and setting yourself up for further injury.

10. Get uncomfortable every day. Living with negative stress is not good for anyone. If something is repeatedly creating anxiety or injury, it may be better to move on. But pushing yourself to improve, even if it's not easy, will be so rewarding in the end. This does NOT mean pushing through pain. It means speaking up if you are in pain, or if you are not ready. It means proving it to your coach if you feel you are ready to progress. It means stepping out of your comfort zone of exercise, to make

yourself better. It means learning everything you can about a new skill, by asking and training your body before you try it. Get comfortable being uncomfortable and you will have an environment for positive stress, which will keep you moving forward.

11. Be BRUTALLY honest about where you are, and your progress will be rewarded. Bragging about a skill that you can't hit 100/100 times and then failing to perform it safely on the field/court/mat are not only catastrophic, but they'll make your coach pull you and put in someone who is if you fail when it counts. So be honest. If you need more practice, figure out a time to be able to practice more. If you don't feel strong enough to try a new stunt/pyramid/tumble pass, etc., being honest about where you are at will help the choreography. If you have a solid foundation, you'll eventually be able to build an even bigger routine.

12. Let go of your old self and ask if you are satisfied with where you are at today. If that injury is still bothering you, dwelling on it will not make it better. Taking action to work with someone who helps resolve injuries will. If you are happy with where you are at, accept it and keep going. If you're not, know that you can always move forward if you let go of what is holding you back. If you cling to the past, you will always be tethered.

13. Lean in. You have the choice to cheer. If you know the risks and still want to do it, lean in, and go for it. Learn

everything you can about everything you want to do. Commit 100% to doing your best, being an exceptional teammate, and to being ok with failing along the way. Commit to getting stronger, improving your mobility and body control, and to listening to your body. Lean in to learn how to do that if not. Lean in and all around you will lean right in with you.

14. Be resourceful. If you aren't making the progress that you want to make, what can you do to improve? There is so much information out there today. If something isn't working, be resourceful and try something different. If you don't feel like your rehab professional is helping you, reach out and find someone who looks at things differently. If you're frustrated because you are not doing what you want in a routine, what do you need to do to be in that spot? Believing in yourself and working toward your goals isn't easy. It won't be handed to you on a platter. But if you can be resourceful, you can find the answer to any problem, and this will make you succeed like nothing else.

"To be yourself in a world that is constantly trying to make you something else, is the greatest accomplishment." Ralph Waldo Emerson

I believe we all need daily reminders to avoid comparing ourselves to others, both as individuals and as a team. I encourage all of you, whether currently cheering, coaching, or parenting, to go into cheer season with a commitment to yourself. You will do your absolute best. You will only look to be better today than you yourself were yesterday. You will admire others for their skills and will learn from them, but you will not compare yourself to them. Visualizing yourself hitting a stretch double as you're working up to doing a stretch will teach your brain that it can achieve a goal. In that visualization, work on FEELING what it is like to achieve this amazing feat. Staying true to your goals and your vision, while not comparing yourself to others will help you achieve and progress so much faster. And the feeling of accomplishment that occurs when you do finally hit that goal will be 10x better.

FUELING FOR PERFORMANCE

Nutritional habits may be one of the biggest factors in keeping ourselves healthy and it's an area that is frequently overlooked. It goes hand in hand with exercise to maintain a healthy body composition.

My mother was diagnosed with Multiple Sclerosis when I was a year old. She struggled every day until I was about 9 years old, when her best friend convinced her to try an alternative treatment method that involved changing her diet. She did some crazy fasting and suddenly she was able to be more present for us with less flare ups. That change completely changed how my family ate. Instead of Ring Dings and Sugar Smacks, we started eating brown rice casserole. She opened the first health food store in our area in 1980 and called it Tidd-bits. (If you follow me on social media, you'll know that is the inspiration for my weekly Thirsty Thursday Tidd-bits of Knowledge ☺) I remember a time we went to a local festival and sold avocado sandwiches. It was challenging because we definitely did not fit in, but looking back, I think my mom had a future thinking vision and gave us all the gift of health that lasted a lifetime.

I was certainly not a full-on follower of my mom's health food 'kick'. I wanted to fit in. In high school my lunches consisted of Tater Tots with mustard and strawberry ice cream bars. Man, I still crave them today! In college, I was in heaven when my dorm cafeteria had a soft-serve ice cream bar, that allowed me to have it covered in 'healthy' granola...let alone the late-night cheesesteaks, pints of ice cream and pizza.

While I never really had a problem with weight, I did always struggle with feeling like I was fat and overweight. My mom used to apologize to me for me 'getting her thighs' after she just complained about having big legs. I wanted to be a top-level flier, and thought if I could just lose 5 pounds, maybe my coach would put me on top. Little did I know that I was probably middle range weight wise on the team, and if I had better strength and body control, and had I looked less scared, I may have been able to be the top.

I first started making myself throw up when I was in my 3rd year of college. I can't remember why I did it. I just knew that I had eaten more than I wanted, and I needed to get rid of it. I started taking No Doz on one of our away trips, so that I would have more energy and burn more calories during our pre-game practice. I was incredibly lucky that I didn't make this a habit. Deep inside me, I knew that this was not the way to control my weight, nor my energy.

After I stopped cheering, I quickly put on 10 pounds. I wasn't on the go as much and I was still eating the same amount that I would eat when I was practicing all the time. I maintained that weight (128 pounds) until my late 30's. I did drop to 114-my high school weight- the week I got married, but again, that was because I was stressed out and didn't eat at all.

The last time I forcibly made myself vomit, I was on a ski trip and had eaten a lot of pasta. I knew it was time to quit that and get a grip when I told my friend that I had made myself throw up, and their response was "Good. You should have because that was a gross amount of food you ate." This was after I had been coaching and one of my girls was anorexic.

When I got pregnant, I put on nearly 20 pounds in 3 months. I didn't feel right. I wasn't overeating, but I had a lot of fluid retention. Perhaps this is why I miscarried…I'll never know. After I lost the baby, I was able to get myself back to 135 and I felt amazing. I was in a smaller dress size; I had energy, and I saw muscles that I always dreamed of. I was able to maintain this for a year before I bumped back up to pregnancy weight. Now that I've hit menopause, it's harder to maintain.

Why do I share all this personal angst with weight? Because I know that cheerleaders struggle with body image issues. I am right there with you. I cringe now when I see this on TV. I look back and wonder why I was so concerned with what other people thought of me? Why did I tie my self-worth to what I weighed? Why did I think that I could control my weight with drugs and vomiting?

My wish-and my own goal now-for all young women and men who struggle with eating disorders and poor self-body image is that they recognize their worth from the inside and not by measure on the scale. That they see how good it feels to be strong. To have energy. To live a vibrant life. To embrace the goodness of good quality food eaten at just the right amount.

Yes, it feels amazing to look at ourselves naked in the mirror and think 'damn, I look good'! It also feels amazing to realize our body is capable of so much more when we take care of it from the inside vs how it looks on the outside.

My mom is a visionary. She went from feeling fatigued all the time and sometimes unable to get out of bed to chasing after 3 young kids trying to keep them in line. I have learned to forgive her for her fat-shaming words in my youth. It was what she knew. I have also learned that I need to be happy and comfortable in my body, and to express that, so that others will see how important it is to love ourselves for who we are, not what we look like. Every day, we learn and grow. That is the beauty of being human.

I am not a Nutritionist nor a Registered Dietitian. This part of the book is only meant to provide guidance for your nutritional needs. Everyone's needs are different, and not everyone responds the same to all food. Today, we have increasing food allergies and sensitivities that limit what people can eat. You may be vegetarian or vegan, pescatarian, or even a fruitarian. There are different diets: macrobiotics; Keto; Mediterranean; Paleo; Gluten-free…the list can go on.

I do believe that food is fuel. We need fuel to keep our bodies running optimally. If we don't have enough fuel the system shuts down. If we have too much fuel, we have a harder time moving. Food provides our muscles with what they need to properly contract and thus is directly correlated to strength.

When we take in less calories than we expend, we lose weight. Eating disorders can lead to the loss of menstruation in females, bone density loss, low blood pressure and heart rate which can lead to dizziness and falls, decreased muscle strength, low testosterone in males, skin, and hair changes. It's extremely important to teach our athletes that their worth on the team is NOT valued by the number on the scale, but rather how strong, energetic, and mentally prepared they are. The ability to perform and stay healthy is what increases their value. And this is done by eating the right amount of food for our energy needs.

Macronutrients

There are 3 macronutrients that are important for athletes to be aware of. These are carbohydrates, proteins, and fats. All 3 are vital to providing a healthy environment for our body to function. These are easy to track yet will vary per each athlete's individual needs.

Carbohydrates in recent years, carbs have gotten a bad rap. Carbohydrates are essential in providing energy and fuel for our body. There are simple carbs and complex carbs. Simple carbs break down into glucose quickly, while complex carbohydrates break down slower. Glucose is the main source of energy and is transferred from the blood to our cells via insulin. Simple carbs will be transferred quicker and have a less sustaining effect while complex carbs will provide energy over a longer period. Stating all carbs are bad is a misconception. There is a big difference between simple carbs such as candy bars, high fructose corn syrup foods, potato chips, sugary drinks like soda, and fruit juices and complex carbs such as whole fruits, whole grains, oatmeal, beans, and vegetables. Generally high fiber foods will also create a longer satiety and thus help us keep the quantity under control as well. I believe that we encourage our athletes to eat a diet that includes more whole vegetables and fruit. If they can eat grains, stick to whole grains like oatmeal and brown rice and avoid simple sugars like candy and soda. I believe we can decrease our risk of Type 2 diabetes if we do this, and we will have athletes who are happier and more energetic on a whole. (Precision Nutrition Encyclopedia of Food, 2023)

Fats

Fat is making a comeback! Healthy fat that is. This doesn't mean deep fried things like chicken fingers and French fries, but rather things like olive oil, avocados, and nuts. Fat is also a primary source of energy for our body. Unhealthy fats or excess will be stored in the body and not broken down into glucose. Just enough healthy fats will break down and promote good energy stores to keep us moving. Fat also helps to keep us warm, helps hormones regulate the body and allows the body to absorb other nutrients. Our athletes need to start to be aware of the difference between saturated and trans fats which increase bad cholesterol (LDL and triglycerides), and we want to limit unsaturated fats which increase good cholesterol (HDL). Finding a balance, with an emphasis on unsaturated fats will promote an overall healthier functioning body. (Association, 2020)

Protein

Protein helps the body to recover and heal. It is made up of amino acids and promotes a building block for bone and muscle growth. It helps our hormones and enzymes to help keep our body functioning properly. For this reason, it is important to get enough protein in our diet. However, too much protein can contribute to an excess in amino acids, ammonia, and insulin, and may cause kidney dysfunction in people with impaired kidney function. In this category are lean meats such as chicken and fish, as well as legumes and nuts and protein powders. (Precision Nutrition Encyclopedia of Food, 2022)

Putting the macros together

Many foods have a crossover in macronutrients. Getting to know food labels will help you understand this more. Knowing how much fat, protein and carbohydrates are in a certain food will help keep track of your daily needs. The right amount needed for each macronutrient will depend on the athlete, but a general rule of thumb is 40% carbs/30% protein/30% fat. For more information I would recommend following www.precisionnutrition.com and as always, when in doubt, check with your physician or a registered dietitian for more guidance.

UNLOCKING MOBILITY, FLEXIBILITY, STRENGTH, AND STABILITY FOR PEAK PERFORMANCE

Coaches and cheerleaders alike frequently say they want to improve their flexibility so that they can have better jumps or be a better flyer, but I've learned over the last 10 years that flexibility is more about the length of the muscles. To have good control with jumps and have higher jumps or to have a prettier heel stretch and scale you need to have good mobility through your joints and muscles as well as stability and strength to perform the act. Improving flexibility by stretching alone will not help.

To have good mobility of our joints and flexibility of our muscles, we need to move our body in the normal 3 planes of motion. There's forward and back (sagittal plane), side to side (frontal plane), and rotation (transverse plane). To develop stability and motor control, we need to train our body to move efficiently through those planes of motion with every action we take. This is most evident when we walk. Every step we take, each joint in our body moves through these motions. Only when we are standing still, are we holding a position. Doing a static stretch is not as effective as dynamically moving in and out of a position to really improve both mobility and stability. Most traditional stretching exercises focus only on static stretching (holding one position) in one plane of motion.

Ankle mobility is important as a cheerleader because it creates power through your legs to propel you into your jumps and tumbling, while also providing a base of stability for balance. As a coach, I used to always cue my teams to point their toes. We'd work the motion of plantarflexion (pointing toes) but did not focus on improving dorsiflexion. Creating length in a muscle and opposite movement in a joint allows for better shortening contraction. By not working to improve active movement between dorsiflexion and plantarflexion, we were making it harder to point toes when we wanted to see that pretty line in our jumps and stunts.

Balance, from a musculoskeletal standpoint, is a combination of mobility through your joints and ligaments, the feedback that they give your brain, the strength and reflexive stability we generate, where your brain perceives the body to be in space and our motor control center processing that information to course correct. It really is an amazing system to keep us centered and moving forward. If you feel like you don't have good balance, improving your mobility and your ability to move in and out of one position will help.

If we look at the ankle, it needs to be able to point and flex, invert, and evert (turn in and out), and pronate and supinate. Many people come in complaining that their feet are pronated. **IT IS SUPPOSED** to pronate. It's just not supposed to stay pronat**ed**. Learning to move enough through those motions will lead to better active control and less pain or injury.

Stability is our ability to control that mobility. To move efficiently through space, we need to be stable enough to be able to control that new mobility and give feedback that corrects where we are in space. This does require a combination of strength and flexibility and challenging your stability on the ground before you get up in the air will help make a stunt safer when in a base's hands.

In the next chapter, we'll break down what each joint needs to do from prep to extension. Stay with me…it's a bit bumpy, but once you're through it, you'll start to understand why it's important to train each motion. ☺

BUILDING THE FOUNDATION: KEY ELEMENTS OF A STRENGTH & CONDITIONING ROUTINE

*Warm-up*s

 I think, and hope, by now most people have gotten away from just static stretching before they get into their jumps or tumbling practice. Research has shown that static stretching decreases our ability to build strength and may set us up for risk of injury. This doesn't mean that we don't do static stretching ever but before a workout or weight training session we need to do more of a dynamic warmup to prep our joints, muscles, and other structures for the activity we are about to do. This includes practice.

 I recommend static stretching first, such as straddle stretches, hip flexors and splits and then transitioning into your dynamic warm up. This will get the blood flow going and start to incorporate stability along with mobility. I start all warm-ups with a breathing exercise to not only help to improve focus before practice, but it also is a baseline core activation exercise. Once you've connected with your breath, working on improving flexibility of the muscles that you'll be using is important. In cheer, we benefit from warming up the hamstrings, the adductors, and the hip flexors. Some exercises that I like to do are bridges, to help activate your glutes; a dead bug exercise with legs out straight, to activate the hamstring and the core. Transition to lying on your stomach for trunk extension where, again I'll do a little bit of breathing some head nods: up and down and side to side, to get your neck warmed up. Then, on to hands and knees do some rocking with the knees apart followed by a frog stretch. Crawling, inch worms and the world's greatest stretch (which includes stretching your hamstrings, hip rotators, hip flexors and spine) are all excellent ways to increase the heart rate, loosen muscles and activate the core. In half kneeling, we can warm up the ankles, the hip flexors, and the glutes. Finishing in standing we can further work on ankle and hip mobility while creating stability in the knees and core. Through each phase of training, our athletes can be aware of their body position by teaching them to move through full ranges of movement without pain, and then finding a neutral position they can maintain will help improve proprioceptive awareness. This is key for any injury prevention or return to sport routine.

A warmup shouldn't take more than 10 minutes once everyone knows the routine.

Strength, agility, and balance.

I frequently hear females shy away from doing any kind of resistance and strength work, because they're afraid of getting big muscles. However, it's important to build strength in order to prevent injury. If our joints and muscles move and work the way they are meant to, we can adapt to different stresses on the body such as catching and landing cradles, holding a person overhead, flipping, and twisting and creating power. You know. All the things a cheerleader does.

There are 7 normal movement patterns that are essential strengthening: core (front and back); squat (knee dominant); deadlift (hip dominant); push (push up or an overhead press); pull (row or pull up); lunge and a carry (Farmers/suitcase, overhead and rack carries which involve carrying a weight in different positions). I like to incorporate both double leg and single leg and arm exercises into the workout routines I create, because it challenges your body in a little bit different way and it will help with balance throughout the body. It's also important to do the exercises in different planes of movement. A side lunge vs rotational lunge vs front lunge, etc.

In addition to the strength exercises, training agility (ladder drills or any footwork and eye-hand coordination exercise) and power (plyometrics such as box jumps or ball slams) are also important. This will build stamina and strength for all aspects of a cheerleading routine.

Strength work should be done three to five times per week, alternating what you do each workout. I encourage a whole-body workout three times a week during the offseason. Preseason and during season, the training should vary because the stressors on the body will be different, but it is still important to maintain strength training throughout. If you do 3-4 sets of each of the above exercises and superset them, the workout will flow nicely. A full workout, including warm up, conditioning and cool down may take 60 minutes.

On days when you are really short on time, take 5 minutes to warm up, 10 minutes to circuit through the 7 exercises as many times as possible, and 5 minutes to stretch at the end.

Conditioning and cardiovascular

Cardiovascular activity is important in any healthy workout routine. I can still remember the first time running the competition routine full out. I was so out of breath. It felt like forever before I was ready to do it again.

The efficiency of our cardiovascular system determines how healthy our heart is. It is key to building stamina and endurance for our daily life. In cheer, we need to be able to do 2 minutes and 30 seconds of full-out, hardcore, high intensity work. Training at high intensity is most important during the off-season. This is the time to do interval training with the heart rate to 85-90% of your max. This will train your heart to work efficiently and effectively and will carry over into the season. 2-3 times per week, for 10-15 minutes, AFTER a strength workout are easy to incorporate. Doing a strength routine as noted above will also help build overall endurance at a lower intensity, which will help with the longer practice times.

High intensity workouts might include kettlebell swings paired with planks; burpees paired with mountain climbers and jumping rope; or sprinting. You would do varying intervals: 30 second work/30 second rest; 45 second work/15 second rest; 2-minute work/1-minute rest; 20 second work/10 second rest.

For strength work, it's important to be consistent for about four to six weeks with one routine while you build your weight up through that time.

With cardiovascular conditioning, it's OK to mix it up. You can change what you're doing every workout as long as you get your heart rate up into your target zone. Lower intensity work, at 65-80% of your max, such as taking a walk, can be done every day.

Taking the time to build cardiovascular endurance throughout the year will not only have a positive impact on the team's performance, but it will also have lasting effects as cheerleaders move into non-cheer life.

Time away from sport

I understand that cheerleading, like many sports, is now a year-round activity. The downside to this is they are missing out on training their body in various ways, which will help to reduce injury in the long run.

In addition to varying time with lifting heavy weights and activities such as cheerleading, is important to your body recovery. It helps muscles to have time to rest and recover. When we are constantly doing the same thing repeatedly it puts the same repetitive strain on our body which contributes to overuse injuries. As much as we enjoy the activity, it's important to take time off from the sport. That time off may be doing something else and letting your body learn a new skill that doesn't involve the same movements as cheerleading. You can still train and do more intensive strength training during the off season, you'll just be using the muscles differently than you normally do in cheer.

I recommend anyone younger than 15 or 16, to do a different sport altogether, for at least one season. This is important because not only will the athlete develop other skills that will carry over to cheer, but this allows the body to rest and recover from the demands of just doing one sport.

Playing a sport with a ball will increase eye-hand coordination. Track will help with endurance and puts a different strain through the joints and muscles that will carry over to cheer. The summer is a great time to do something that you don't do regularly throughout the year such as swimming or kayaking.

Recovery and cross-training will help prevent overuse injuries, as well as mechanical injuries that may occur with distraction. This means we do need a day off in training through the week. If your normal routine is to lift five times a week, do a high intensity workout two or three times a week and then run two days a week for your cardiovascular, it's important to have a day fully off. Instead try doing something to exercise your brain; or do yoga; or just a casual stroll to appreciate the world around you. Just do something that's completely different and allows your body to just take that time to recover and rest.

Side note*** I do understand that most athletes stay with their sport year-round, and many young athletes don't play multiple sports these days. I understand that from a logistical standpoint, however I do think this sets kids up for a bigger risk of injury. This is why I will continue to encourage extended time away from the sport. I don't see it changing anytime soon, but as coaches, I do think it's important to recognize how we are limiting our athletes' overall development. This is not specific to cheerleading. Soccer, dance, gymnastics, and baseball are all well known to encourage year-round play for their athletes.

When we talk about strength and conditioning, the time that you take off is just as important as the time that you train. When prepping for a competition or even the first game, we tend to push to get it all done: learn the routine; build on skill technique; train endurance; do it again until it's perfect. We get mid-way through a season, and everything starts to fall apart. Injuries occur. The team is stressed and fighting. Our skills decline instead of moving ahead. And we push more.

In Massachusetts, we have a rule that you can't practice more than 6 days a week. This is a start. I encourage all of us to schedule rest periods within those allotted practice/game times as well. Our bodies just cannot sustain a constant push all the time. This doesn't mean drop your practices to once a week. It does mean that we need to pay attention to what our athletes are demonstrating. If stunts are starting to fall a bit more or if form is declining, it may be a sign that the team needs a break. Alternating intensity between practices can help greatly to reduce an injury. Maybe on Tuesday you go all out with the routine a bunch of times. Wednesday might be more of a walk through, or better yet, a visualization day.

Another option would be to create a ritual of active recovery between run throughs. Have each cheerleader visualize how they did in a section, then have them visualize how they would correct it. Do this once through the whole routine and then actually run full out again. Or if you have someone who needs to work on flexibility, taking an active rest to work mobility between sets can be a great way to increase flexibility and actively recover. The key is, allow the heart rate to come down, let muscles rest and allow overall tension to decrease.

Sleep

We need to sleep. Everyone is different but we generally need six to nine hours per night. Studies show that going to bed at the same time and getting up at the same time promotes a better sleep environment and helps people to sleep better. Having a sleep routine such as turning electronics off an hour before bedtime, doing your dishes or planning your lunch right before you go to bed and doing things that are calming, allows the body to relax to help get you ready for sleep. Sleep is important in helping your body recover. Not only that, but it also helps us to be more alert, so we are able to adapt better to changes in a routine, or in a movement. Whereas if we are tired, you're not able to be as quick at catching a stunt or watching out for somebody who's doing a tumble pass right next to you. Being well rested really helps your body to function at its most optimum, including getting better grades.

Starting each day with a self-assessment will provide a starting point for what you're able to do in a workout. Teaching your cheerleaders to do the same will help them give you feedback for what they need more-or less- of. it will provide a framework for how to progress skills. In this section, we'll run through a self-assessment of your static posture, a gross movement screen and a more specific assessment of the pelvis, ribs, spine, and head.

You can use a mirror to help you see your position, but it is also good to feel where your body is in space. This will help you learn both on the ground or while in the middle of a routine.

Static posture

My mentors (Gary Ward and Chris Sritharan) from Anatomy in Motion (https://findingcentre.co.uk/) recommend doing these observations while in your underwear and in a mirror. Minimal clothing and a mirror are optional. Cheer practice gear will work fine. =D

Start by checking in with your feet. Where are your foot pressures? Do you feel more pressure in the ball of your feet or the heels? On the inside of your feet or outside? Is it the same on both feet?

Next let your hands rest on your hips. Feel the bones in the front (the ASIS), are they even? Now slide your thumbs to the back of the pelvis at the 'dimples' (the PSIS), are they even? From the side, is the ASIS even with the PSIS? Is it the same on each side? Is one ASIS more forward than the other?

Looking at your shoulders from the side, are they stacked directly over your hips or are they more forward? Are they even side to side? Is one higher than the other?

Next, where is your head? Is your chin more up or down? Are your ears lined up over your shoulders? Are you tipped to one side or the other?

Make note of these spots. You can reassess after a workout or the end of the day. Note any improvements or changes. Ideal static posture will set your body up to perform and move optimally. This means if you draw a plum line from your ears to your outside ankle (lateral malleolus) you should be in a straight line if looking from the side. If you're looking from the front, everything should be level. If you look from above your head, shoulders, and pelvis should be even. The most important check-in will be with the feet.

When our body is aligned at rest, we have equal weight between toes and heels. There is equal pressure between the knuckle of your big toe (first metatarsal joint), the knuckle of your little toe (fifth metatarsal joint) and mid-lateral (outside) of your heel.

This is an easy check-in to do throughout the day. By making small adjustments in our feet, we can greatly affect postural line up in the joints above.

Gross movement screen

The Functional Movement System changed how I evaluated people. It connected the dots for assessing motion and finding out what is needed to help my clients progress. This section is a combination of the Functional Movement Screen and the Selective Functional Movement Assessment. You can learn more about the system at https://www.functionalmovement.com

This portion of the movement screen is where we will look at everyday movements that indicate what your body is missing and needs further attention. To ensure you do this the same way each time, start with your feet together. This section will discuss what your body is meant to do. The corrections will come later.

Trunk flexion-Bend forward towards your toes, while keeping the knees straight. Note what it feels like and if you can do it with knees straight and head down. Do your hips shift backward and does your back flex (round)? Return to center. Note* If not, you have some restrictions that need to be addressed.

Trunk extension-Bend backward with arms overhead, keeping knees straight. Again, note what it feels like. Do your hips move forward as your trunk and shoulders move back? Are you able to keep your arms straight and are your hands moving past your shoulders? Do your shoulder blades move past your hips? Do you hinge at your lower back or is there a smooth curve from your lower back to your upper back? Return to center. Note* If not, you have some restrictions that need to be addressed.

Trunk rotation-Twist your body to the right and then to the left. Pause at the end of each direction to note what it feels like. Do you move evenly in both directions? Do your feet stay in one position? Does your hip and knee extend and externally rotate on the side you're turning toward?

Overhead squat-Start with your arms overhead in a narrow 'high-V', and your feet slightly wider than hip distance apart. Keeping toes pointing straight forward and your heels flat, squat as low as you can without pain. Do your chest and shoulders remain upright, or do you fall forward? Can you get your bottom to your feet? If you see any variations, go to ½ kneel (see below)

Shoulder Overhead Mobility-In one motion, reach one arm over your head to touch the opposite shoulder blade. Head remains forward and your shoulder does not shrug

Shoulder Behind Back Mobility-In one motion reach one arm behind your back to touch the opposite shoulder blade. Your palm remains facing away from your body, your head stays forward, and your shoulder blade flat against your rib cage.

Single leg stand-Start with feet together, lift one knee like a 'lib'. Do your hips stay level? Does your kneecap and front of thigh stay facing forward or does it turn in or out? Does your foot stay relatively neutral, or does it wobble a lot? Repeat on the other leg. If you see any variations on either leg, go to ½ kneel.

½ kneeling Start with your feet together. Step forward with one foot and go down onto the back knee. Let your back toes relax. Does your knee line up directly under your hip? Do you tend to lean forward or back? Can you keep the front/lower part of your ribs down? If the answer is yes, you likely need to work on your ankle mobility or stability vs your hip. If not, you likely need to work on the hip.

Rotary Stability- Start on all fours with your hands directly under your shoulders and your knees directly under your hips. In one motion reach your opposite arm and leg out straight and return to start. Repeat opposite side. Can you do this with your hips level? Does your back stay straight? Is it the same on both sides? Variations may mean that you need hip or posterior core stability.

Push-up- Starting on the floor with your thumbs in line with your chin, lift your elbows toward the ceiling, and your knees off the floor. In one motion, push your body away from the floor. Can you do this and maintain a straight spine or does your back arch? If not, you may need shoulder and core strength and stability.

Trunk Rotation

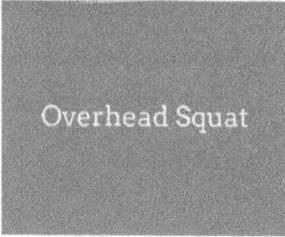

Overhead Squat

Trunk Flexion

Trunk Extension

Single Leg Stance

1/2 Kneel

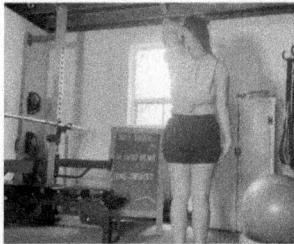

Behind Head

Behind Back

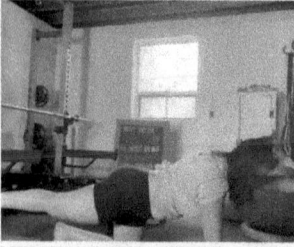

Rotary Stability

Push Up

These movements happen with every step we take. In breaking down stunts, we can use these movements to help us determine where someone is in need of better movement and avoid just cranking on a joint trying to get it to move. When your hip moves forward into flexion, your pelvis will posterior tilt.

Your pelvis mimics what your ankle does. It's difficult to break down every movement of the ankle but learning what is missing in movement from your pelvis, ribs and head. (They move in the opposite motion from each other) can provide you with a lot of information to help you stunt better. If a flyer is struggling with single leg balance, or a base or tumbler struggles with chronic ankle sprains, looking at the pelvis will provide a lot of information to tell you which plane of motion is in need at the ankle and foot.

Again, doing the assessment in cheer shorts and sports bra will show limitations better. (And thus, a way to correct the deficits.)

Try each movement on the ground. Then in sitting and standing.

Pelvis

Anterior/posterior pelvic tilts-Anterior tilt-starting with your feet hip distance, tip your ASIS toward your toes, like you are trying to get your butt to look like a Kardashian's butt. Return to center. Posterior tilt-tip the ASIS up toward your belly button. Which way is easier, which is harder?

Hip hike/drop-With feet hip distance apart, heels flat on floor, bend one knee and feel your same side hip drop down and the opposite hike up. Does it feel the same on both sides? Is there any pain?

Shift-With feet hip distance apart, allow pelvis to shift to the right 'like you are hip checking the wall to your side." Keep your knees straight. Do your shoulders tip slightly away, or do you have to move your shoulders to get your hips to move? Does it feel equal on both sides? Where do you feel it?

Pelvic rotation-With feet together, twist your pelvis to the left and then to the right. Keep your hands on your chest and face forward. How does it feel? Is there a difference? Is one way easier than the other?

Anterior Pelvic Tilt

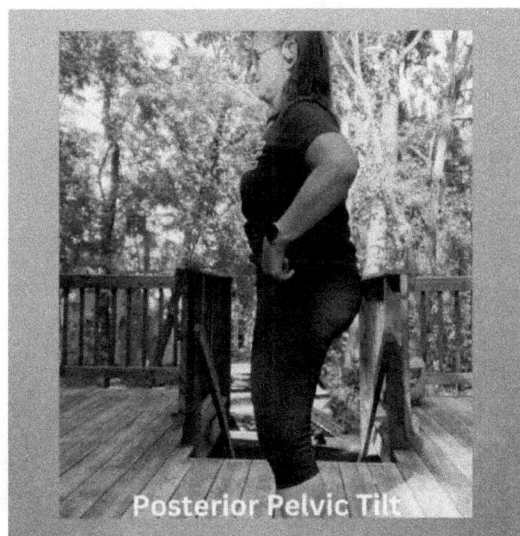

Posterior Pelvic Tilt

Pelvic Hike/Drop

Pelvic Shift

Pelvic Rotation

Ribs

Anterior/posterior tilt-Keep your pelvis still, lift your sternum toward the ceiling for a posterior tilt. Bring the ribs down toward your belly button for an anterior tilt. Note the difference.

Side bend-Lean shoulders to one side. Can you lead with your upper body and allow your pelvis to shift, or do they have to move together? Is it equal on both sides?

Shift-Imagine your rib cage is resting on a table. Keep your pelvis still and slide the ribs to one side. Return to center. Try the other side. Is it equal? Can you do it? (PS…. if you were a dancer, these are rib cage isolations 😊)

Rotation-Keep your hips facing forward and turn your shoulders to the left. Return to center. Then rotate to the right. Note the difference. Is there pain? Is it equal?

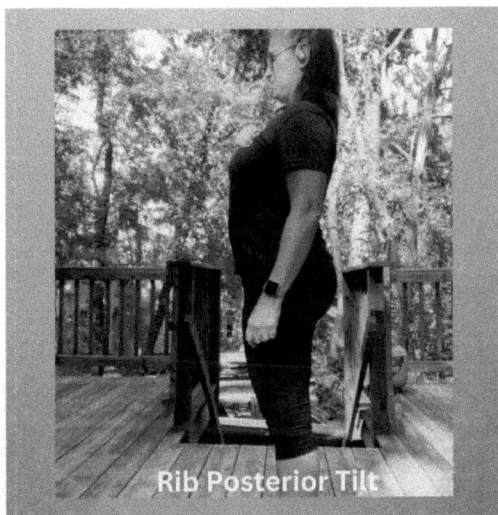
Rib Posterior Tilt

Rib Anterior Tilt

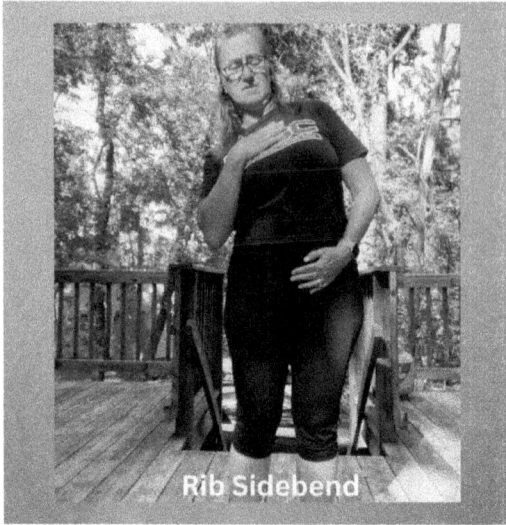

Rib Sidebend

Rib Shift

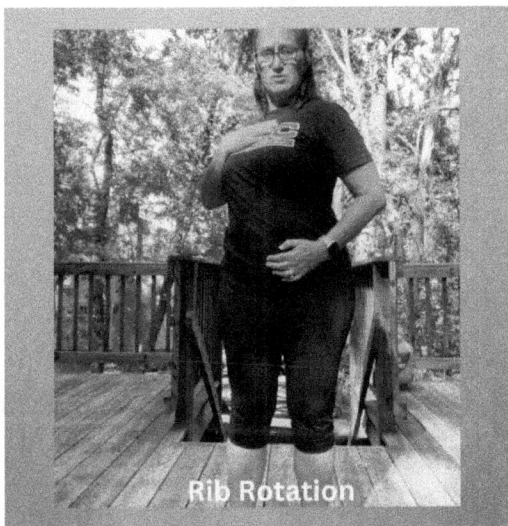
Rib Rotation

Head

Anterior tilt/posterior tilt-pull your chin straight back like you're making a double chin. Return to center. Then allow your chin to move forward like you're sticking your neck out. Which way is easier? Which is harder? Can you move easily in both directions?

Side bend-tip your left ear toward your left shoulder. Come to the center. Tip to the other side. Is it equal? Can you do it without moving the rest of your body?

Shift-Now imagine your chin resting on a table. Slide your head to one side. Come to the center. Assess the other side. Can you do it equally to both sides? Do you have any sticky points?

Rotation-Turn your head to one side. Stop in the center then turn to the other. Note the differences.

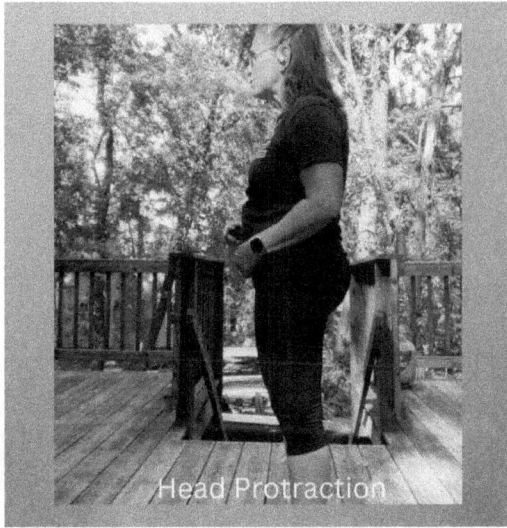

Head Protraction

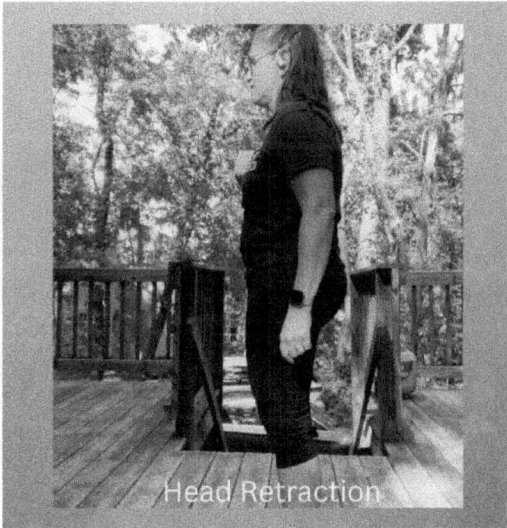

Head Retraction

Neck Flexion

Neck Extension

Neck Sidebend

Neck Rotation

*Note: I don't have a picture of neck shift, because it is a sticky point for me, and I couldn't get a clear picture ☺

What does it all mean?

These assessments are meant as a starting point. They are positions that we move in and out of all the time. The purpose of this book is not to teach how to correct movements. Rocky Snyder, a Certified Strength and Conditioning Specialist recently authored a wonderful book called Return to Center (Rocky Snyder, 2020) that breaks down movement a bit more. He includes workouts to do when one movement or another is 'missing', and I highly recommend it to program more specifically based on your individual needs.

The exercises and workout routine below are meant to be generic. If you can't perform it correctly and without pain, find a different one. If you continue to get stuck, find a qualified movement professional to learn a better way. If you're unsure if something is right for you, you can always go back to the self-assessment to check if it's improved or not. The key to moving better, getting stronger and improving your cheer skills is **listening and learning** how your body moves and what you feel as you are doing any task.

STRENGTH IN MOTION: EXERCISES TO SAFEGUARD AND ELEVATE YOUR PERFORMANCE

In this chapter we get into the good stuff. We start with the warmups, advance to strengthening and finish with conditioning. But first...let's talk about timing and programming.

Did you know that our workouts need to change frequently for our muscles to continue to develop? We see quick adaptations and neurological changes when we start a program but after 4-6 weeks, those begin to slow. So, making changes every month or so will ensure continued strength changes and progress.

It is also important to vary workouts depending on where we are in a cheer season. The workouts we do while we are in season should be different, because of the demands on the body, than pre or post season. According to the National Strength and Conditioning Association's guidelines these training cycles would be broken down into preseason, in season, active rest/post season, and the off season. Each cycle would last 4 weeks, with 3 weeks of ramping up and one week of de-loading. (Baechle & Earle, 2000)

Preseason is the time to increase intensity of sport specific drills. For cheerleading this would be increasing lower body plyometric exercises, like squat or box jumps, to help with jumps and tumbling, and upper body plyometrics, such as overhead ball tosses or ball slams, to help with catching and tossing. It is the time to build strength and to work on shorter, high intensity workouts. Strength workouts are generally 3 times per week for about 1 to 1 1/2 hours and aerobic conditioning would be on non-resistance days for 45 minutes to an hour. For a high school team, preseason would be roughly from the end of June through mid-late August.

In season, is a time to maintain what we've built. Workouts should be 1-2 times per week for about 30 minutes. Intensity should vary between high intensity, core, balance, and agility exercise. For those who cheer for two seasons, this may start in September and go through to March.

Post season is the time for active rest which is when the body can recover and heal from the hard work and stress of the season. Lower intensity workouts, which use different muscles than when cheering, are beneficial. This is a great time to encourage different playful and recreational activities such as swimming and hiking. Workouts are lighter and may include circuit training and light jogging or cycling. The post season could last from the last competition in March through the first or second week in May.

Off season, which varies per cheer team, is the time to find out what the athlete's starting base- line cardiovascular fitness is like. During the off season you will increase intensity with the focus on increasing resistance training. Workouts may include 4 days of strength training, as well as aerobic conditioning on the off days. This will help improve overall fitness along with body composition. (Baechle & Earle, 2000)

Mobility work can be included in both a warm-up and a cool down for each workout at any time throughout the year.

As you can see, the volume, intensity and intention throughout the year needs to vary. Doing this will ensure safe mobility, ongoing strength gains and along with proper nutrition, a well-maintained and healthy physique. We all want to look good in our uniforms or just our clothes, but this should not be the only goal. Getting and keeping our bodies healthy, fit, and able to move comfortably throughout life is a much bigger goal.

In the next sections we'll talk about the different components of a workout. The exercise specifics are in the chapter to come.

Warmups

The purpose of a warmup routine is to prepare the body for the work it's about to do. This means the muscles, the joints, the connective tissue, and the brain. You can use the same warm up for practice, games, or competitions, but incorporating a mixture of exercises that take your body through multiple planes of motions will assure you keep moving efficiently.

Strength training

There are 7 fundamental movement patterns that we do every day that are important to include in a strength training routine.

Knee dominant I recently finished a 50 squat per day for a 5-day challenge in the Healthy Cheerleading Facebook group. I started the week before talking about ways to improve squat technique and then the challenge consisted of 50 bodyweight squats over the next 5 days. At the end, I was asked the question as to what is the difference between a squat and a lunge? And do we need to do both if they work the same thing? I would argue that although they work the same muscle groups, they do so in different ways, and therefore both are equally important. If you are short on time, choosing one is ok, but if you are an athlete (aka someone who moves), it's important to incorporate both (as well as a hip hinge pattern where the hip moves more than the knees) into a well-rounded strength and conditioning program. Of course, there are some prerequisites for that are important to consider as you develop your training program.

Both squats and lunges are fundamental movement patterns that we do every day. Moving from sitting to standing is a squat pattern. Getting up and down from the floor requires a lunge pattern, or if you are not doing that regularly, one can argue that walking has components of a lunge pattern too. Both squats and lunges will work the entire lower body and core. A lunge pattern requires a bit more stability in the gluteus Medius and quadratus lumborum to keep the pelvis level than the squat because it is a transitional movement pattern where you shift from one foot to the other. For both, you need sufficient ankle, hip and thoracic (upper back) mobility to perform correctly. If we move too much in these areas, we may lose stability and form. If we are stiff and don't move enough through these joints, we may compensate with excess knee or lumbar (low back) movement. The difference, and why we need to work both, is in the stability and motor control that each movement allows.

A squat pattern is one of our first developmental patterns that occurs as we learn to walk. We first roll, then press up to quadruped (hands and knees), start to rock (a non-standing squat) and crawl, then come to our heels. If you've ever watched a baby who is starting to pull to stand, they will inevitably let go of the surface they've held onto and settle down into a full deep squat. This position at the bottom of the squat is much easier to control than standing at first for them. And the mobility of a full squat is something we lose as we age. Training the full squat pattern will help improve that mobility and will build symmetrical strength that allows us to stand in place on 2 feet. Of course, to do this effectively one may need to break down the squat and work up to improving what is missing so that it can be done with good form (top of thigh to parallel, chest upright with ribs down and chin tucked, neck long). Being able to squat is a precursor to any jumping exercise, such as jump squats and box squats, etc. This will create explosive power which will help cheer jumps be higher. It is also the position needed for a load in position with 2 legged stunts.

The lunge pattern is important in training deceleration of movement. This is important for any activity that requires you to land (a jump; go downstairs; step off a curb or walk down a ramp), stop, or change direction. Training a lunge can help develop single leg strength which a squat cannot do. Lunging will help to develop coordination of movement, challenging both the brain and the body to make the movement happen. This can help improve balance and weight shift needed for any upright activity. Lunges are the precursor to cartwheels and round-offs too.

Some will argue that being able to lunge is a precursor to a squat because you need to develop hip and ankle mobility and control first. I think both are important and it will depend on your own mobility and stability that will determine which area you need to focus on first. I also know from experience that if your big toe mobility is limited, you will have trouble executing a lunge, vs if your ankle mobility is limited you may have more trouble with a squat. Finding what is missing and working drills to improve them will not only help you perform the motions more effectively and safely, but it will feel better too. (And yes. There are ways to modify both to be able to incorporate the patterns into your workouts)

The bottom line: training both squatting and lunging and learning to do them both correctly, without compensation and/or pain is important. There are many exercises that can help to train these and seeking help to find out what is best for you would be beneficial. In addition, I would encourage a true single leg squat as well as lateral or rotational lunges to include all our normal movement patterns. This doesn't mean we add a ton of exercises into our loaded strength routine, but perhaps we include some into a warmup routine or a conditioning routine, or one month do a forward motion, the next a side movement or rotational movement. The key is to get a variety of movements into your day and explore the movement when you are able, to assure you can access full mobility without pain and with good mechanics. If you do this, I expect you will feel stronger, move easier and will feel more balanced overall.

Hip dominant

A hip dominant exercise puts more emphasis on the posterior chain, aka the glutes and hamstrings. This movement requires that we bend at the waist by hinging at the hip. The knees will be slightly bent, but the primary movement is at the hip. This is extremely useful to prevent back injuries and to help us pick up objects correctly off the floor. Having powerful glutes and hamstrings will help prevent knee injuries as well as create the strength we need to sit into the set position of a handspring, lift someone into a stunt, and create stability for those who fly.

I encourage both double and single leg exercises in a well-rounded workout routine. This will help improve core strength, balance, and will help isolate strength in the hips. Training bilateral or single limb work also helps the body show any imbalances. It also helps to train the body to avoid compensation with anti-rotation momentum.

Push

Pushing movements are things we need to do in daily life: push a shopping cart, move furniture etc. In cheerleading, we push people overhead. We also push the ground away from us in any tumbling activity where the hands are in contact with the ground. A well-rounded workout will include both horizontal pushing (such as a bench press or a push up) and vertical pressing (such as an overhead shoulder press or handstand pushups).

To execute pushing motions correctly, we must look at what the core is doing. If in a handstand or push up the lower back is hyper-extended and the pelvis more anterior tilted, it will cause a compressive movement on the lower back and possibly pain. This may happen if someone doesn't have upper back mobility and core stability when they press. Or they just may not have the best body awareness and motor control to be able to hold a more centered position. In either case, modifying the press is important so as not to put more strain through the lower back and shoulders. This could mean working on more high planks or elevating the hands for a pushup. It could also mean doing a landmine press, which involves pushing a bar in a diagonal, overhead; or performing a press in ½ kneeling until the postural cues can be maintained. This will give you a great idea on if someone is ready to progress their basing skills: if they cannot press a weight overhead with good postural alignment, how will they do if they are pressing a moving body overhead?

Pull

Again, we pull all the time in daily life: opening doors, picking things up from the floor. In cheerleading, we may build a stunt from the ground in which we need to pull the body towards us. Unfortunately, we tend to do more pushing than pulling and with the amount we sit through the day, our pulling muscles tend to get under used. This can cause trouble if our scapula (shoulder blade) stabilizers aren't doing their job efficiently when we are lifting overhead. Both the rotator cuff and muscles that control how fast the shoulder blade moves need to be working at just the right time and amount to prevent shoulder impingement when we lift overhead.

Performing single and double arm rows both horizontally and vertically will help to train the pulling muscles. A great whole-body and core exercise that we also consider a vertical pull, is a pull up. With both the horizontal and vertical pulls, keeping our chin tucked, back of the neck long, ribs/xiphoid process down and pelvis stationary will build a solid foundation for the pulling muscles to perform optimally.

I think pull ups are one of the most beneficial exercises that we can do, however, they are also one of the hardest to do correctly. It's been my experience that females have a harder time as well. This is why it's important to program some variation into a well-rounded workout. Does this mean every athlete must crank out 10 full out, hanging pull ups to be considered fit? No. There are modifications for everything. Starting where the athlete is at, building proper mobility and strength, and progressing when and if they are ready will set them up for success and limit the risk of shoulder injury.

I believe including more pulling exercises, which are performed correctly, than pushing exercises in a workout program can help to reduce shoulder and neck injuries.

Carry

A carry is just what it sounds like. As with all the above, we carry things every day: groceries, books, our laptop bag. In cheerleading we carry differently in a rack (prep level), waiter (transitional level above shoulders), or overhead (extended) position. Bases need to be able to control these positions with good positioning before adding a moveable body to them.

We, of course, also need to work on carrying both with 2 arms (a farmer carry) and with one arm (a suitcase carry). We can also mix it up with carrying the weight at chest height (rack carry), with our shoulders raised to 90 degrees (waiter carry) or overhead. All must be done with good postural alignment.

Including carries in your workouts will help work both the front and back core. It is great for training the shoulders to be down and back and we use the cues to push the weight toward the floor, in a suitcase or farmer's carry, to help with that. Doing a rack, waiter or overhead carry will challenge the shoulder and scapula stabilizers. All carries when done correctly will help reduce the risk of back, neck and shoulder injuries.

Aerobic vs Anaerobic Cardiovascular Conditioning

Aerobic conditioning can be defined as "any exercise that can be maintained over a period of time, utilizing big muscle groups and is rhythmical in nature." (Harsh Patel, 2017) Generally, using the Karvonen formula and maintaining a target heart rate of 60-80% of our max heart rate (HR) (220-age), for 30 minutes or longer is thought to work aerobic conditioning. This may include activities such as running, dancing, or cycling.

Anaerobic is defined as "intense exercise for a shorter period of time" (Harsh Patel, 2017). To work on improving anaerobic conditioning we would work at 85-90% of our max heart rate, for shorter periods. High intensity interval training has become very popular these days. This anaerobic conditioning may mean anywhere from 10 seconds to 3 minutes of work followed by 10 seconds to 3 minutes of rest.

Both aerobic and anaerobic conditioning have benefits in overall cardiovascular health and fitness. They utilize our energy systems differently, and in a general strength and conditioning program a workout should include both. Weight training is a form of anaerobic training for most people. Including a short, 10-minute round of HIIT at the end of a strength workout is beneficial. On non-strength days I recommend a combination of aerobic and anaerobic work, depending on where you are in your training cycle.

Cheerleading utilizes more of our anaerobic system. With competitions being full out for 2:30 minutes, at high intensity, we need to be able to access anaerobic energy more than aerobic energy. Yet training both is important. To get through a 2+ hour practice, cheerleaders will need to have sustained energy with short bursts of higher intensity work. As we talked above in periodization, the off-season is a great time to build both aerobic and anaerobic capacity. During the pre-season and in-season periods, train more anaerobic conditioning and in the active rest period, train lower intensity aerobic conditioning.

Cool downs

I am struggling to write this section. I think it's because in my own workouts, cooling down is the first thing I tend to let go. I use all my allotted time to work out and then skip a cool down process. In doing this, I'm missing a key component of a healthy body. Taking time to cool down allows our muscles and joints to relax; it returns our nervous system to a parasympathetic state and aids in overall recovery. Developing a cool down routine that you or your team does, post-workout, post-practice, and post-game will make this important step a habit and will help improve mobility, flexibility and thus help to improve jumping and stunting skills.

There are some key motions that will benefit from cooling down after a practice or game. Including mobility for the hip flexors, hamstrings, quads, and calves are important for the lower body; pectorals, triceps, and wrists for the upper body; and spinal cogs for the spine and skull.

It's important to walk around a bit to let your heart rate return to a lower rate before you lie down. This goes for after performing a routine full out in practice too. Instead of lying down, a combination of standing stretches and slow dynamic stretches will help the body start to cool down effectively. I recommend exploring the motions instead of doing a prolonged hold. This will encourage joint mobility as well as muscle flexibility, and since you are moving through motion vs holding static, you are at less risk of losing the strength you might during a static stretch.

Start in standing and let the heart rate come down and then move to lying down to do some static stretching, spinal cogs and then back into stand for some gait base standing exercises again will help the motor control system remember the newly gained mobility from stretching. This only needs to take 5-10 minutes, and it will keep your body feeling good after.

The next chapters will provide you with an example of exercise routines to build strength, improve mobility and flexibility and promote an improvement in skill level too.

BLUEPRINT FOR SUCCESS: DESIGNING EFFECTIVE EXERCISE PROGRAMS FOR CHEER ATHLETES

In this section we will put exercises together to create a program for you. The intensity and volume will vary depending on what 'season' you're in for training.

Planning your workout based on when you want to peak is called periodization. What does that mean for cheerleaders, as well as adults who don't participate in competitive sports anymore?

Periodization is the process of scheduling your workout routines to build skill, strength, power, conditioning, and body composition. Our bodies change when we change up our routines, whether that be for weight loss, building mass or building strength. Yes, it's important to be consistent. This means doing our workouts regularly and maintaining a healthy diet most of the time. However, to see regular changes, we need to mix up the types and intensity of our workouts, and in doing this our intake and nutritional needs will change too.

As a cheer coach, I didn't fully understand these principles. I knew my team needed to get stronger in general, but I didn't give them good structure in their workouts that went with the principles of periodization. Perhaps incorporating these principles into our workouts would have set them up for less risk of injury and better progression of skill.

How does periodization work? If we look at a high school or college cheer program as a model, we will break the year of training into 4 parts. Preseason (July-September) we will increase the intensity of sport specific training and include more strength, power, and higher intensity conditioning. In season (September-March for 2 season cheerleaders), we want to maintain what we've built, with less frequent resistance work and more focus on agility, balance, and skill. An active rest period (March- April) allows time for the body to recover both physically and psychologically. This should include lower intensity and lower volume work that may include other recreational activities. The off season (May-July) is the time to build a baseline of cardiovascular and resistance training while working to improve body composition. The time frames would vary for All-star programs, but the principles will be the same.

The other key component of training is adaptation. Our body will adapt to what we do. Usually, it takes about 6 weeks to make a true body change, so changing a workout every 4-6 weeks is also important. The type of exercises may stay the same, but the sets, reps and intensity may vary depending what season you are in.

Of course, a daily mobility routine, proper water intake, a diet based on minimal sugar and junk food, and adequate rest are also important to help you achieve your goals.

I hope this provides a guideline for the importance of changing your routine periodically no matter where you are in your fitness goals. If you are currently cheering, using these guidelines can help to build strength, maintain body composition, and improve your skill level. Having a regular strength and conditioning routine, doing daily mobility work, eating foods that fuel vs depletes your body, and finding periods of active rest as well as sleep, will not only help reduce injuries, but will allow for quicker progression of skills.

Example of seasonal workouts

Pre-season: focus on sport specific conditioning. *Train 3x/week. Off days can be steady state (walk, run, cycle, hike, etc.) cardiovascular exercise for 30-60 minutes, warm-up and flexibility work daily.*

- Warm-ups: pick 10; 5 reps each.

- Plyometrics: Pick 1 lower body and 1 upper body exercise. Do 3 sets of 5.

- Strength: 3x/week; 2 sets of 10-12 reps; pick 2 exercises from each category that you alternate per workout (i.e., single leg deadlift day 1; 2 leg hip lift day 2; single leg deadlift day 3.). Stay with these 2 for the season.

- Conditioning: Mix and match. One day do 5 rounds of Tabata with 5 different exercises (4 minutes of 20 seconds' work:10 seconds rest for 8 rounds); the next do

30 seconds on: 30 seconds off; then 2 minutes work:30 seconds; or do a circuit of all 10 exercises 45 seconds on:15 seconds off and 1 minute rest between rounds, for 3 total rounds.

- Flexibility: 30-60 seconds of each exercise 1-2 times

In-season: focus on agility and balance; 2x/week strength exercises **either after practice or on off practice days**; warm-up and flexibility work daily.

- Warm-ups pick 10; 5 reps each.

- Agility: Pick 2. Do 3 sets forward and back.

- Balance: Pick 2. Do 5 times for each.

- *Strength:* 1-2 sets; 12-15 reps pick 2 exercises from each category that you will alternate per workout (i.e., split squat day 1; box squat day 2) Stay with these 2 for a month then pick 2 other exercises in each category for the next month.

- *Flexibility:* 30-60 seconds of each exercise 1-2 times

Active rest: keep intensity and volume low.

- Continue with warm-up routine and flexibility exercises.

- Get outside and play!

- Try a yoga class.

- Dance to your favorite songs

- This is a great time to try a new activity such as Animal Flow https://animalflow.com/ or Zumba.

Off-season: The time to build; work on body composition; test strength and cardiovascular system…aka the time to PUSH! Moderate to higher intensity steady state workouts 2 days; 1-day lower intensity work-flexibility routine or yoga class or casual walk

- *Warm-ups* continue as above.

- *Plyometric:* 3 sets of 5; pick an upper body and 1-2 lower body that you will alternate

- *Agility:* Pick 2

- *Strength:* 4 times/week. Pick 2 exercises for each category that you will alternate workout1/workout 2. Stay with the same exercises for 4-6 weeks, then change. For the first 4 weeks do 3 sets of 8 repetitions; the 2nd month do 5 sets of 5-6 repetitions; and the 3rd month do 6-8 sets of 3-4 repetitions. As your rep range decreases, your load/resistance should increase.

- *Conditioning:* Mix and match. One day do 5 rounds of Tabata with 5 different exercises (4 minutes of 20 seconds' work:10 seconds rest for 8 rounds); the next do 30 seconds on: 30 seconds off; then 2 minutes work:30

seconds; or do a circuit of all 10 exercises 45 seconds on:15 seconds off and 1 minute rest between rounds, for 3 total rounds.

- *Flexibility:* 1-2 sets of each exercise for 30-60 seconds each.

All the following exercises are included in the accompanying PDF's and YouTube videos.

Warm-ups: Pick 8-10 exercises per workout. Vary the exercises with each workout, so that you include all of them throughout the week. Start lying down. End with standing. Do 5 repetitions each.

1. 90-90 breathing

2. Crocodile breathing

3. Supine spinal cogs

4. Hip circles knee bent.

5. Hip circles knee straight.

6. 2-legged bridge

7. Single leg bridge

8. Bridge with march

9. Quadruped rock

10. Quadruped adductor rock

11. Bird dog

12. Quadruped cogs

13. ½ kneeling ankle mobility

14. ½ kneeling hip flexor mobility

15. Inch worm

16. World's Greatest Stretch

17. Spiderman

18. Standing hip hike/drop

19. Standing hip shift

20. Standing spinal twists

21. Walk backwards hamstring.

22. Walking step forward/sit back.

23. Walking open gate/close gate

24. Walking Frankenstein

25. Backward lunge with reach

26. Forward lunge with twist

27. Alternating side lunge

28. Bounding

29. Skipping

30. Cross connects.

Plyometrics and Agility

Always work on quiet landings. *Choose one upper body and one lower body plyometric per workout. Do 3 sets of 5. Low volume/high impact.*

Lower body plyometrics:

1. Jump squat.

2. Box squat

3. Alternating lunge

4. Skater lunge

5. Squat to box jump

Upper body:

1. Push-ups (start at wall, lower surface as you get stronger)

2. Med ball slams

3. Squat and throw.

4. Med ball toss to a partner or at a wall

5. Power drop with Med Ball

Agility drills

1. Ladder In-in/out-out forward

2. Ladder in-in/out-out ladder

3. Shuffle sticks wide.

4. Cross behind stick

5. Ladder scissor drill

Balance

1. Clock step stationary leg stays straight.

2. Clock step stationary leg bends and straightens.

3. 3-D hamstring

4. Standing forward bend clock

5. 3-way step up

Core

Pick 2 exercises per workout.

Planks

1. Quadruped plank

2. High plank

3. Plank on elbows

4. Plank with leg raise.

5. Plank with arm reach

6. Plank drag through.

7. Side plank on knees

8. Side plank legs extended.

9. Side plank with arm reach

10. Side plank with leg raise.

Anti-Rotation

1. Russian twist

2. Belly press

3. Chops

4. Lifts

5. Landmine Oblique Twist

Dead bug variations

1. 90-90 Leg lower knees bent.

2. 90-90 Leg lower knees extended.

3. Hands on wall leg lower

4. Dying bug

5. Leg lower with weight in hand

Strength

Knee dominant

1. Box squat

2. Goblet squat

3. Split squat

4. Sumo squat hold

5. Single leg squat to box

Hip dominant.

1. Single leg deadlift

2. 2 leg hip lift

3. Single leg hip lift

4. Kettlebell/dumbbell 2-leg deadlift

5. Slider leg curl eccentrics

Push-vertical

1. ½ kneel single arm shoulder press

2. Tall kneeling alternating arm shoulder press.

3. Standing single arm press

4. Standing alternating arm press

5. Handstand push-ups at wall

Push-horizontal

1. Straight arm hold

2. Hands elevated push up

3. Push up.

4. Alternating dumbbell bench press

5. Dumbbell bench press

Pull-Vertical

1. Supine pulldown hollow hold with stick

2. Chin up with band

3. Chin up

4. Cross arm pulldown with band.

5. Cross pull down with triceps extension.

Pull-Horizontal

1. Cat-cow

2. Bench row

3. Inverted row

4. ½ kneel single arm row

5. Standing single arm row

Conditioning

1. Get up/get back down.

2. Mountain climbers

3. Plank with leg to side

4. Body weight squats

5. Jump rope.

6. Jumping jacks

7. Med ball slams

8. Burpees

9. Sprints

10. Alternating step ups

Flexibility/Cool-down

1. Spinal cogs-supine, quadruped, standing.

2. Heel strike

3. Suspension/propulsion forward

4. Suspension/propulsion to the side

5. 3-way hamstring

6. ½ kneel foot to butt

7. Seated wide angle pose.

8. Warrior 3 with support

9. Chest shoulder opener with hands clasped.

10. Criss cross 3-way shoulder and hip

You can find videos of all these exercises and more by scanning the QR codes below.

STRENGTH AND
CONDITIONING FOR
THE CHEER
ATHLETE

Excel Spreadsheet

Excel Spreadsheet With Full Workout

STRENGTH AND
CONDITIONING FOR
THE CHEER
ATHLETE

Mobility and Flexibility Playlist

Strength And Conditioning For The Cheer Athlete

STRENGTH AND CONDITIONING FOR THE CHEER ATHLETE

Warm Up Exercises Playlist

Warm Up Playlist

If you have questions about the exercises, or any content in this book please reach out to me at Laura@MoveBetterLLC.com.

CONCLUSION

Cheerleading is a sport that has been progressing faster than the speed of light. People are noticing and we are making strides towards the whole world recognizing us as a full-on sport. And to paraphrase Voltaire and Uncle Ben from Spiderman…" with great progress, comes the need for great responsibility". To be mindful of how we move, to build strength and conditioning, and to do the work it takes to keep us progressing.

The exercises and content in this book have come from my own experience and learning. The exercises I included are by no means exhaustive. There is still so much more I want to learn about human movement and strength. I hope that is the same for you.

Please explore various movement and exercise specialists. Find what works for you.

Always keep learning. Ask questions. Listen not only to the people you learn from, but to your athletes.

Coaches, embrace the parents who bring their athletes to you.

Parents respect the experience of the coaches who care for your athletes.

Cheerleaders, put your whole heart into your sport. Keep pushing. Understand when your parents get upset, over anything you might think is silly. Listen and learn from your coaches. They love you just like you were their own. And will have your back for as long as you need and want it.

My journey in cheerleading has been a blessing. I love seeing the progress we are making as a sport. I am so grateful that the sport I love gave love back to the career I chose. And I look forward to continuing to help you enjoy the cheer ride for as long as you want, while being strong, healthy, and happy along the way.

CONNECT WITH LAURA

If you would like to work with me, have a free consultation, connect on social media or access any of my free guides and workout plans here are all the ways to connect.

- *Join our Personal Training Programs*

  https://movebetterwithlauraturner.com/personaltraining

- *Centered: A mini course to help you improve posture, balance and how you move*

  https://movebetterwithlauraturner.com/centered825932

- *Take the Injury Prevention Challenge* https://ltthecheerpt.com/injurypreventionchallenge
- Access the free guides and connect with LT on social media www.LTTheCheerPT.com

Please note, this book is not meant as medical advice. If you have an injury, you need to follow up with your local physical therapist and/or physician.

As with any exercise program, this is just your starting point. As you progress and get stronger you will need to challenge your routine. I encourage you to continue to learn and experience movement. Over time, I hope you fall in love with moving and stay in love with cheer for life.

I started writing this book with everyone else, during the pandemic in 2020. It has taken me this long to get this written and finished. Call it procrastination or fear of completing a project of love, it is what it is.

I did the formatting on my own. My sister edited the first draft and caught some big errors along with jogging my memory about things we both experienced through cheerleading. I did the final editing. Please excuse any grammatical errors, spacing issues or just weird layouts. As I tell everyone, as a cheer coach I was great at seeing the big picture. I am not the one you want to clean up a routine. My assistant coaches were amazing at that. Right now, I just want to get this book into the world. The big picture will have to do. Thank you for understanding.

Some things have changed since the time I started working on this project.

For instance, Concussions are one of the highest injury occurrences now. Musculoskeletal injuries are also high. And sadly, cheerleading has the highest catastrophic injuries for female athletes, and RED-S (Relative Energy Deficiency in Sports). (Xu AL, 2022 Jan 18)

RED-S is something I am just learning about but includes energy deficiency for all genders. Symptoms include fatigue, rapid weight loss, dysmenorrhea, low libido, frequent illness and more. You can learn more on the Boston Children's Hospital Website www.childrenshospital.org/conditions/reds (Program, 2005-2024)

The world, like cheerleading, is ever changing and there is always something to learn and grow from. Don't wait like I did to complete this book.

Take a chance. Go now. Learn how to lift and move and get ready to cheer. Stick with it for as long as you can. Embrace the challenge and enjoy the ride.

Cheers to you for taking a chance on my ideas and for taking the first step with buying this book!

Much love,

LT The Cheer PT.

I must give a big shout out to Keyonni Adams, who is the athlete in my videos. Key is an amazing physical therapist and strength coach herself and she graciously volunteered to be my model. You can connect with her on Facebook and give her a shout out at

https://www.facebook.com/liftingforwomen

Greg Todd and the SSHC Team, Gary Ward, David Weinstock, Kathy Dooley, Perform Better, Gray Cook, and Mike Boyle changed my life. I was ready to give up on physical therapy and working with people. If I hadn't attended their courses and programs, I am not sure what I would be doing now.

I fell in love with cheerleading when I was 14 years old, thanks to many friends who made it fun for me at Bethlehem Central High School. If not for them, this book would never be thought of.

My coach at Northeastern, Lorrie Wright, gave me wings. She pushed me to be better, taught me how to laugh at myself and ultimately was the model for whom I learned to coach.

My teammates were my best friends then and truly made cheering a family. My partners through the years encouraged all us flyers, to get into the weight room and start building strength. From them, my love of lifting began.

I coached from 1997-2012. The kids who cheered for me, their parents, and my assistant coaches, at all levels will forever hold a piece of my heart. I learned so much from them that I don't think they ever knew. They gave me the opportunity to not only be a coach in a sport I love, but they, and their parents, have become my friends. I don't think I can ever express my gratitude enough that they have been in my life.

My nieces and nephews Cameron, Brendan, Erin, Lexi, Morgan, Maddie, Mason, Kaela, and Trevor. They light up my world and make every day worth living. My wish for them is that they keep chasing their dreams and never give up.

My mom, dad, sister, and brother have always encouraged and supported me. They put up with my practicing routines at all hours. They talk me through crises all the time. My sister, Jenn, is always my other set of eyes when it comes to my vision of a routine and the writing of this book. My brother, Shawn, supports me in everything I do. Whenever I need an ear, he is always there. My dad teaches me every day how to be patient and to listen. My mom shows me every day what hard work and commitment to health looks like. The fun we had dancing around our living room or doing skits for holidays for sure influenced my choice of sport and spotlight. They mean the world to me.

Bill, my husband, is my rock. He showed up at games when we first started dating and my heart flip flopped more than me doing a torch flip at nationals. And it still does. He has shown me what it means to be committed to health and fitness. He pushes me to be better. And even though he doesn't quite understand my obsession with cheer after all these years, he has shown me what it takes to stick with something for the long haul.

REFERENCES

1. Association, A. H. (2020, October 21). Heart.org. Retrieved from heart.org/healthy-eating/eat-smart/fats/dietary: https://www.heart.org/en/healthy-living/healthy-eating/eat-smart/fats/dietary-fats#:~:text=Dietary%20fats%20are%20essential%20to,Your%20body%20definitely%20needs%20fat.

2. Baechle, T. R., & Earle, R. W. (2000). Essentials of Strength and Conditioning. Champaign: Human Kinetics.

3. Boyle, M. (2004). Functional Training in Sports. Champaign: Human Kinetics.

4. Boyle, M. (2010). Advances in Functional Training. Aptos: On Target Publications.

5. Cheerleading Safety Data and Research. (2020, July 22). Retrieved from www.usacheer.org: https://www.usacheer.org/safety/research

6. Cook, G. (2003). Athletic Body in Balance. Champaign: Human Kinetics.

7. Cook, G. (2010). Movement. Aptos: On Target Publications.

8. Dooley, D. K., Folckomer, D. A., & Quirk, D. (2019). Immaculate Dissection II: Dissecting the Lower Extremity.

9. Harsh Patel, H. A. (2017, February 26). World Journal of Cardiology "Aerobic vs anaerobic exercise training effects on the Cardiovascular System". Retrieved from

NCBI.nlm.nih.gov:
https://www.ncbi.nlm.nih.gov/pmc/articles/PMC5329
739/

10. Hill, N. (1937). Think and Grow Rich.

11. Larson, S. (2020, July 27). onefunnelaway.com. Retrieved from PT-M1: You must believe: https://onefunnelaway.com/challenge

12. Laura Turner, P. D., & Jeananne Elkins. (2016). Rise Presentations. Retrieved from Northeastern University: https://www.northeastern.edu/rise/presentations/chee rleading-injuries-can-the-risk-be-reduced-via-movement-screening-and-appropriate-exercise/

13. Lockett, S. (2018, August 17). 5 ways to get fit and into cheerleading shape. Retrieved from www.blog.omnicheer.com: http://blog.omnicheer.com/post/5-ways-to-get-fit-and-into-cheerleading-shape

14. Lucas, G., Kasdan, L., & Yoda. (1980). Star Wars Episode V: The Empire Strikes Back Movie.

15. Merriam Webster/dictionary. (30, July 2020). Retrieved from www.meriam-webster.com: https://www.merriam-webster.com/dictionary/handspring

16. Physical Therapy Guide to shoulder Labral tear. (2011, September 6). Retrieved from www.choosePT.com: https://www.choosept.com/symptomsconditionsdetail /physical-therapy-guide-to-shoulder-labral-tear#:~:text=Traumatic%20labral%20tears%20usually

%20occur,to%20experience%20traumatic%20labral%2
0tears

17. Piper, W. (1930). The Little Engine That Could. Platt &
    Munk.

18. Precision Nutrition Encyclopedia of Food. (2022,
    January 31). Retrieved from
    https://www.precisionnutrition.com/encyclopedia/foo
    d/protein:
    https://www.precisionnutrition.com/encyclopedia/foo
    d/protein

19. Precision Nutrition Encyclopedia of Food. (2023, March
    30). Retrieved from Precision Nutrition Network:
    https://www.precisionnutrition.com/?s=carbohydrates
    +

20. Richard, L. (1966). Good Golly Miss Molly.

21. Rocky Snyder, C. (2020). Return to Center, Strength
    Training to Realign the Body, Recover from Pain, and
    Achieve Optimal Performance. Herndon: Mascot Books.

22. Ryan Maciel, R. P. (2020, July 30). Precision Nutrition
    Principles of Nutrition. Retrieved from
    www.precisionnutrition.com:
    https://www.precisionnutrition.com/principles-of-
    nutrition

23. Spine-health.com. (2020, November 3). Retrieved from
    Spine Health: https://www.spine-
    health.com/glossary/pars-
    interarticularis#:~:text=Pars%20interarticularis%20refe
    rs%20to%20a,to%20a%20condition%20called%20spon
    dylolysis.

24. Staff, M. C. (2019, January 8). Healthy Lifestyle Fitness. Retrieved from Mayo Clinic: https://www.mayoclinic.org/healthy-lifestyle/fitness/in-depth/overuse-injury/art-20045875#:~:text=An%20overuse%20injury%20is%20any,much%20physical%20activity%20too%20quickly.

25. Step by Step: Bump and go lib , pop cradle. (2019, September 6). Retrieved from www.americancheerleader.com: https://www.americancheerleader.com/bump-go-lib-pop-cradle/

26. Tina. (2016, July 25). 3 ways to work through an unexpected cheer injury. Retrieved from blog.omnicheer.com: http://blog.omnicheer.com/post/3-ways-to-work-through-an-unexpected-cheer-injury

27. US Dept of Health and Human Services, C. o. (2010). Facts about concussion and brain injury. Retrieved from www.cdd.gov/headsup: https://www.cdc.gov/headsup/pdfs/providers/facts_about_concussion_tbi-a.pdf

28. Ward, G. (2013). What The Foot: A Game Changing Philosophy of Human Movement Eliminating Pain And Maximising Human Potential. London: Soap Box Books.

29. Program, W. T. (2005-2024). *Relative Energy In Sports*. Retrieved from Childrens Hospital: https://www.childrenshospital.org/conditions/reds#overview

30. Xu AL, B. J. (2022 Jan 18). Understanding the Cheerleader as an Orthopaedic Patient: An Evidence-Based Review of the Literature. *Orthop J Sports Med*.

www.ingramcontent.com/pod-product-compliance
Lightning Source LLC
Chambersburg PA
CBHW071226090426
42736CB00014B/2982